Preface

"The best way to predict the future is to invent it." — Alan Kay

In the vivid landscape of digital marketing, where the sands are ever-shifting beneath our feet, there lies a profound opportunity cloaked within the complexity of Meta's advertising ecosystem. This book is a robust compass designed to help you navigate through the labyrinth of algorithms, targeting options, and content strategies that define the Meta universe.

Our journey begins with unraveling the intricacies of direct response advertising, setting the stage for a deeper dive into mastering the art and science behind successful campaigns on platforms like Facebook and Instagram. We'll explore the alchemy of appealing visuals, persuasive copy, and strategic targeting to captivate your audience. Each chapter serves as a stepping stone, building upon the last, to elevate your Meta ad mastery from a foundational understanding to executing campaigns that not only meet but exceed your marketing objectives.

The impetus for this journey unfolded through countless interactions with digital marketers and business owners, who, like you, were navigating the choppy waters of online advertising. Picture Lucy, a passionate owner of a burgeoning online boutique, who struggled to break through the noise on social media. Or consider Mark, a digital marketer at a tech startup, juggling the ever-changing ad formats and privacy regulations in his quest to scale their online presence. Their stories, and many others, resonated deeply with me, stirring a desire to create a guide that demystifies the nuances of Meta advertising and paves a straightforward path to success.

Affectionately referring to industry pioneers, the latest research, and the rich tapestry of my own experiences navigating the Meta platforms, this book is a labor of love and a testament to the collaborative spirit of the digital marketing community. I am deeply indebted to the many hands and hearts that have shaped its content, offering their insights, critiques, and encouragement along the way.

To you, the reader, I extend my sincerest gratitude for choosing to embark on this journey with me. Your dedication to mastering your craft is a powerful testament to the unwavering spirit of curiosity and growth that defines the best of digital marketing. This book is specially tailored for digital marketers, small to medium-sized business owners, and anyone with a spark of interest in online advertising who is familiar with the basics but seeks to navigate the complexities of advertising on Meta with greater ease and effectiveness.

As you flip through these pages, I invite you to embrace the challenges and opportunities that lie ahead with an open mind and a resilient spirit. Remember, the aim is not just to ride the waves of change but to steer with confidence toward uncharted territories, where the true potential for innovation and growth lies.

Thank you for your purchase, and without further ado, let's set sail toward conquering the vast expanse of Meta advertising together, unlocking secrets, and achieving direct response success that outwits algorithms, outmaneuvers competitors, and outperforms expectations.

Chapter 1: The Power of Direct Response in the Digital Arena

Amelia sat at her desk, the glow from the computer screen casting a sterile light across her features. She was locked in a silent dialogue with her thoughts, the cursor on the screen blinking like a steady heartbeat in a room where time seemed to pause. Around her, the office hummed with the subdued chatter of colleagues, the occasional clack of keyboards punctuating the air like distant thunder. She had been here before, at the cusp of decision, the precipice of action, her marketing campaign poised like an arrow drawn back in the bow.

Her mind wandered to the visuals of the ad she had designed, the punchy call to action that would compel viewers to pause their scrolling and engage. Direct response advertising was not just a strategy; it was her spear against the mammoth that was market apathy. She knew that on platforms like Facebook and Instagram, the immediacy of a user's interaction could be harnessed, delivering them from mere viewers into active participants. This was the heart of her craft, the drive behind each carefully placed word and image.

The faint aroma of air-conditioned sterility was suddenly cut by the soft scent of someone's lunch, a homemade curry that carried with it an exotic verve. It was home and a world away, a gentle reminder that outside these glass walls life thrummed with a million different flavors. Yet here she was, trying to capture elusive attentiveness in the vast digital landscape. Could she spark the longing for a product with the same ease that this aroma evoked hunger?

Metrics would tell. The numbers were like a constant murmur in her head, figures she would soon pore over to discern the secret paths through which human attention flowed. Click-through rates, engagement levels, conversion percentages; these were the runes she read to foretell success or forecast the need for change. The campaigns of the past whispered to her, tales of soaring numbers and other times when expectations fell like Icarus from the sky. This time, she vowed, the sun would not melt her wings.

Her finger hovered over the 'Launch' button. There was no orchestra to swell at this moment of triumph or potential disaster, only the thrum of blood in her veins and the silent roar of possibility. She clicked, and the ad burst forth into the digital wilds, a crafted message in a bottle set adrift in the vast ocean of content. Now came the watch, the wait, the meticulous adjustment of sails to harness the wind of consumer desire.

As the screen before Amelia declared her campaign live, one

cannot help but wonder, when does the essence of direct response advertising transcend mere analytics and become a bridge between desire and fulfillment?

Unleashing the Might of Direct Response on Meta Platforms

Direct response advertising stands as a backbone in the digital marketing world, especially within the bustling ecosystems of Facebook and Instagram. To understand its monumental importance is to unlock a treasure trove of opportunities for businesses aiming for precise targeting and immediate customer action. This potent strategy transforms casual browsers into committed buyers, elevating not just engagement rates but also driving substantial conversions.

The essence of direct response advertising lies in its power to **effectively reach and engage a target audience**. Imagine being able to whisper directly into the ear of your ideal customer, delivering a message so compelling it prompts immediate action. This isn't just hyperbolic fantasy; it's the reality of well-crafted direct response campaigns on Meta platforms. By leveraging sophisticated targeting algorithms, businesses can place their ads right in front of those most likely to convert, making every marketing dollar count.

But here's where the true magic unfolds – the ability to **analyze real-time metrics to optimize campaigns** for even better results. Meta platforms offer a granular view of how ads are performing, from click-through rates to engagement metrics. This treasure trove of data is not just numbers on a screen; it's actionable intelligence that, when used adeptly, can fine-tune your marketing messages, target more effectively, and ultimately, unlock higher conversion rates.

Perhaps the most captivating aspect of direct response advertising on Meta platforms is its **dynamic adaptability**. In a digital landscape that's constantly evolving, being able to swiftly adjust your strategy based on real-time feedback is invaluable. It's akin to navigating a boat in turbulent waters with the ability to adjust your sails at a moment's notice to harness the wind most efficiently.

This opening chapter merely scratches the surface of the profound impact direct response advertising can have when harnessed correctly on Meta platforms. As we embark on this journey together, remember that mastering direct response is not just about pushing ads. It's about fostering connections, understanding human behavior, and leveraging technology to not just reach but resonate with your audience.

In the chapters ahead, we'll dive deeper into **strategies for outwitting algorithms**, techniques to **outmaneuver competitors**, and secrets to **outperforming expectations**. Each page turned will bring you closer to becoming a maestro of Meta advertising, capable of orchestrating campaigns that not only capture attention but also capture hearts.

The core problem this book addresses — the complexity and fickleness of Meta's advertising ecosystem — is no small hurdle. Yet, with the insights and strategies laid out in the coming chapters, you'll learn how to dance with these complexities rather than being trampled by them. Harnessing the power of direct response advertising on Meta platforms becomes less of a daunting task and more of a thrilling adventure. One where the prize is not just improved metrics but a deeper, more meaningful connection with your audience.

So, let's turn the page and embark on this journey together. A journey that promises not just mastery of direct response advertising on Meta platforms but a transformation in how you approach digital marketing itself. Welcome to the path of elevating your ad mastery, where every click isn't just a metric, but a step closer to achieving your marketing goals.

Understanding the significance of direct response advertising on Meta platforms is akin to unlocking a high-powered engine in a race car. It's all about optimizing performance, speed, and precision to cross the finish line ahead of the competition. This form of advertising allows businesses to directly communicate with their target audience, encouraging instant actions through their digital campaigns on platforms like Facebook and Instagram. With billions of active users, these platforms offer a fertile ground for businesses to plant their messages and watch the engagement grow.

In the realm of direct response advertising, immediacy is king.

Unlike traditional advertising, which often focuses on brand awareness over time, direct response campaigns are designed to evoke an immediate reaction. This could be anything from clicking a link, signing up for a newsletter, or making a purchase. The beauty of this approach lies in its measurability. Businesses can track the performance of their ads in real-time, tweaking and refining their approach to maximize their return on investment.

Imagine planting a garden where you can instantly see which plants thrive and which struggle, allowing you to adjust their position, water, and sunlight at the moment. This is the essence of direct response advertising on Meta platforms; it's dynamic, responsive, and incredibly effective when executed correctly. By understanding the user behavior and preferences that drive engagement on these platforms, businesses can create targeted ads that speak directly to the needs and desires of their audience.

However, navigating the intricacies of Meta's advertising ecosystem requires more than just a rudimentary understanding of its tools and features. Mastery comes from diving deep into the analytics, deciphering user patterns, and applying these insights to craft compelling ad campaigns. It's about marrying creativity with data, intuition with analysis. Only then can businesses fully leverage the immense potential of direct response advertising to meet their marketing goals.

Understanding the significance of direct response

advertising on Meta platforms is crucial for achieving marketing success, as it allows for real-time engagement and optimization to drive conversions.

Engaging Your Target Audience Effectively

At the heart of direct response techniques lies the art of captivating storytelling. It's not enough to simply present your product or service; you must weave a narrative that resonates with your target audience, making them the protagonist of your story. This approach humanizes your brand, transforming passive observers into active participants. The power of a well-told story can turn indifference into interest, and interest into action.

Engagement is the currency of the digital age. A successful direct response campaign doesn't just reach its audience; it speaks to them, understands them, and offers them something of genuine value. It's about creating a dialogue rather than a monologue. This engagement is quantifiable—likes, shares, comments, and, most importantly, conversions, all serve as indicators of your campaign's resonance with your audience.

Consider the analogy of a market vendor. In a bustling market full of distractions, the vendor must not only catch the attention of passersby but also engage them with compelling reasons why their products stand out. Similarly, direct response campaigns must cut through the digital noise to capture and hold the audience's attention. It's about finding the right combination of imagery, messaging, and timing to create a moment of connection.

To cultivate this engagement, it's essential to segment your audience, tailoring your message to match their specific interests and needs. This segmentation enables a more personalized approach, increasing the relevance of your campaign. By leveraging Meta's robust targeting capabilities, advertisers can reach distinct groups within their broader audience with precision, delivering content that is highly pertinent to each segment.

But reaching and engaging your target audience is only the start. The true measure of a campaign's effectiveness lies in its ability to inspire action. This requires a clear call to action (CTA) that guides the audience towards the next step, be it making a purchase, signing up for more information, or another desired outcome. The CTA should be unmistakable and compelling, acting as the critical bridge between engagement and conversion.

How can we ensure that our messages not only reach our audience but resonate deeply with them, prompting not just a nod of agreement but a step towards engagement?

Optimizing Campaigns Through Real-time Metrics

The landscape of digital advertising is ever-shifting, and

staying ahead entails a continuous process of analysis and optimization. Real-time metrics serve as the compass that guides advertisers through this terrain, offering insights into what works and what doesn't. This data-driven approach empowers advertisers to make informed decisions, enhancing the effectiveness of their campaigns and maximizing their budgets.

Think of it as fine-tuning an engine. Just as a mechanic adjusts various components to optimize performance, marketers adjust their campaigns based on real-time feedback from their audience. This could involve tweaking ad copy, modifying visuals, or adjusting targeting criteria. The goal is to continually refine your approach to better align with your audience's preferences and behaviors.

The beauty of real-time metrics lies in their immediacy. There's no need to wait for a campaign to conclude before gleaning insights. Instead, advertisers can monitor performance indicators like click-through rates (CTR), conversion rates, and engagement metrics as their campaigns unfold. This immediate feedback loop allows for swift adjustments, minimizing wasted effort and resources on ineffective strategies.

Harnessing these metrics requires a combination of analytical skill and creative thinking. It's not just about interpreting data; it's about translating these insights into actionable strategies that enhance campaign performance. Whether it's identifying the most engaging content, optimizing ad spend, or pinpointing the optimal timing for ad delivery, every decision is informed by concrete data.

By understanding the significance of direct response advertising, learning how to effectively engage our audience, and analyzing real-time metrics to optimize our campaigns, we can drive higher conversions and engagement rates, ultimately achieving our marketing goals.

Exciting benefits await you as we journey through the world of direct response advertising on Meta platforms. By understanding the power of direct response in the digital arena, you are unlocking a key that can open the door to unparalleled success in your marketing endeavors. **Reaching and engaging your target audience effectively,** utilizing real-time metrics to optimize your campaigns, and ultimately **driving higher conversions and engagement rates** are the cornerstones of this vital strategy.

As we delve deeper into this book, you will uncover the secrets to outwitting algorithms, outmaneuvering competitors, and outperforming expectations in the ever-evolving digital landscape. By mastering the art of direct response advertising on Meta platforms, you are equipping yourself with the tools needed to thrive in this dynamic environment. So, buckle up and get ready to embark on a transformative journey that will elevate your meta ad mastery to new heights.

Chapter 2: Crafting Personalized Campaigns that Convert

Marissa stood by the wide window, coffee cup cradled in her hands, as the city below her whispered the morning to life. Inside her apartment, the air hummed with the quiet buzz of her digital world—a symphony played on silent keyboards and distant servers. Today, she was to sculpt the currents of data into a form as personal as a whisper in a lover's ear, to touch the life of strangers with the precision of a poet choosing the perfect word.

Her thoughts were scattered, like the myriad pixels on her dual monitors that awaited her touch, a canvas to be filled with visions borne from the numbers and trends compiled over countless nights. She had questioned the impersonal nature of her industry; the billboards shouting into the void, the TV ads missing their marks. Those were the dreams of yesteryear, and Marissa's dreams whispered of something more intimate.

Last night's campaign results trickled in, glowing on her screen as she took her seat. Her eyes traced the data, feeling their siren call. The spike in engagement, the favorable click-through rates. To another, mere percentages. To her, the affirmations of shared humanity reached through the cold ethereal expanse of the internet. She remembered the faces in the focus group and their pleas for relevance, for something that spoke to their lives, their loves, their fears.

Marissa sifted through the demographics, past purchases, preferences, but sought something deeper. Behind each byte of data was a beating heart, a mind that yearned, however unconsciously, to be understood and seen. The city below was more than concrete and steel; it was a living tapestry of souls, and she was unraveling the threads ever so gently.

A chime pulled her from her reverie, a new email from her director. There was urgency in its subject line, a reminder that her daydreams must give way to decisions. But Marissa knew those daydreams were the wellspring of her craft. Her past campaigns loomed in her mind—some soared, some faltered. And from each, she learned the delicate dance between data and the human touch.

The morning was no longer young, and with her coffee now a comfortable warmth in her belly, she began the day's work. What stories would the data tell her today? Which lives would she touch, and how deep would her digital messages engrave themselves upon the canvas of their daily musings?

Would the data reveal dreams she could fulfill, or would it be merely a mirror showing the fragmented reflections of a thousand desires?

The Era of One-Size-Fits-All Is Over

In the ever-evolving landscape of digital advertising, sticking to outdated methods is akin to trying to fit a square peg into a round hole—it simply doesn't work. The rise of data analytics and consumer insights has heralded a new dawn where personalized, data-driven campaigns are not just a luxury, but a necessity for achieving successful direct response advertising. The transition from a broad, catch-all approach to a more targeted, nuanced strategy is crucial in creating campaigns that **not only attract attention but also convert**.

Businesses today have at their disposal an unprecedented amount of data which, when leveraged correctly, can unlock deep insights into consumer behavior and preferences. This treasure trove of information allows advertisers to craft messages that resonate on a personal level with their target audience. Imagine presenting a vegan cookbook to someone who's demonstrated clear interest in veganism online, versus casting a wide net with general culinary guides. The difference in response rates can be staggering.

Yet, harnessing this data effectively requires a fundamental shift in how campaigns are conceived and executed. **Crafting personalized campaigns** demands a keen understanding of audience segments, a creative mindset to tailor messages that strike a chord, and the technical know-how to use advertising platforms to their fullest potential. It's about sending the right message, to the right person, at the right time.

The Art of Personalization in Ads

The key to impactful ads lies not only in the message but in **how well it mirrors the recipient's current needs and desires**. This art of personalization might seem daunting at first. However, by breaking down your target market into smaller segments, it becomes more feasible to craft messages that feel personal and relevant to each group. An essential aspect of this process is ongoing testing and optimization. What works for one segment may not resonate with another, and preferences can shift over time.

Ad personalization also extends to the choice of platforms and formats. For example, a beautifully designed video might captivate a younger audience on Instagram, while a well-crafted, text-based ad could perform better on Facebook among an older demographic. The ability to adapt and tailor not only the message but also the medium, is what separates the good from the great in digital advertising.

Leveraging insights and data does more than just improve the chances of your ad being noticed; it fundamentally enhances the user experience. When consumers feel that a brand understands their unique needs and preferences, it fosters a sense of connection and loyalty. This, in turn, **increases the likelihood of conversion** and encourages repeat business.

Staying Ahead in a Competitive Landscape

In the digital advertising arena, standing still is the fastest way to fall behind. The competitive landscape is continually shifting, with new technologies and changing consumer behaviors creating both challenges and opportunities. Personalized, data-driven campaigns are essential for staying ahead of the curve. They allow businesses to **make meaningful connections** with their audience in a way generic advertising cannot.

Achieving better results in this context isn't just about working harder but working smarter. Advertisers must be willing to embrace change, experiment with new approaches, and continuously refine their strategies based on real-world performance data. The role of personalized advertisements in this competitive digital landscape cannot be overstated. They are the linchpin of a strategy that values quality over quantity, precision over guesswork.

Embracing personalized, data-driven campaigns is not merely a tactical shift but a strategic one. It involves a deeper understanding of your audience, an appreciation for the power of data, and a commitment to continually improving and evolving your advertising approach. By doing so, you can ensure that your message not only reaches the right ears but sings in perfect harmony with the desires and needs of your audience.

Shift from Generic Advertising to Creating

Personalized, Data-Driven Campaigns Tailored to Audience Preferences

In today's fast-paced digital world, the one-size-fits-all approach to advertising is akin to casting a wide net hoping to catch anything that swims. However, with the vast ocean of consumer preferences and behaviors, this method yields less and is cost-inefficient. A shift toward personalized, data-driven campaigns promises a more targeted approach, ensuring that the message resonates with the intended audience. This personalization not only improves engagement rates but also enhances the consumer's experience with the brand.

Imagine you're a tailor in a bustling market, crafting suits without knowing the measurements of the people who will wear them. You make them based on a standard size, hoping they'll fit as many people as possible. In contrast, a data-driven campaign is like measuring each customer beforehand, ensuring the suit fits them perfectly. This is the essence of shifting from generic advertising to creating personalized, data-driven campaigns.

This personalized approach leverages a treasure trove of data - from browsing habits to purchase history, social media activity to consumer feedback. By analyzing this information, businesses can tailor their messages, offers, and even the timing of their advertisements to align with the individual preferences of their target audience. This not only increases the likelihood of conversion but also fosters a deeper connection between the consumer and the brand.

The implementation of personalized, data-driven campaigns requires a mindset shift - from broadcasting a broad message to engaging in a one-to-one conversation with your audience. Businesses that embrace this shift are rewarded with higher engagement rates, increased loyalty, and ultimately, better ROI on their advertising spend. It's about recognizing that in the digital age, the most powerful connection you can make is one that feels personal to the receiver.

The key takeaway is the significance of moving away from generic, one-size-fits-all advertising to embrace the precision and effectiveness of personalized, data-driven campaigns.

Leverage Insights and Data for Creating Impactful Ads that Resonate with the Target Audience

In the realm of digital advertising, data is the compass that guides the creation of impactful ads. The more a business understands its audience, the better it can tailor its messages to meet their needs and preferences. Leveraging insights and data is not just about collecting information; it's about translating this information into a language that speaks directly to the heart and mind of the consumer. This requires a delicate balance between science and art – the science of analyzing data and the art of using this analysis to craft ads that resonate on a personal level.

Consider the data as raw ingredients in a chef's pantry. The chef, much like the advertiser, must decide which ingredients work best together to create a dish (or ad) that will appeal to the tastes of their diner (or audience). They must understand not only what is available but also how flavors combine, how ingredients interact, and what presentation will most appeal. The right combination can turn a simple meal into an unforgettable experience, much as the right combination of data insights can transform a basic ad into a compelling narrative that speaks directly to the viewer.

By analyzing behavior patterns, demographic data, and engagement rates, advertisers can pinpoint what content appeals to different segments of their audience. This goes beyond basic targeting; it's about understanding the nuances that drive consumer behavior. What time of day are they most active online? What types of content do they engage with most? Answering these questions allows advertisers to create ads that aren't just seen but are remembered and acted upon.

Moreover, leveraging data insights enables businesses to test and refine their advertising strategies in real-time. Through A/B testing and analytics, advertisers can continuously improve their campaigns, optimizing for higher conversion rates and better overall performance. This iterative process is essential in a landscape as dynamic as digital advertising, where consumer preferences can shift rapidly.

Yet, with all the talk of data and analytics, it's crucial not to lose sight of the most important element: the human connection. The most effective ads are those that touch on universal human emotions, experiences, and desires. They remind us that behind every data point is a real person.

What if the secret to creating ads that truly resonate lies in viewing every data point as a story waiting to be told?

Achieve Better Results by Understanding the Role of Personalized Advertisements in the Competitive Digital Landscape

In the digital age, the battleground for consumer attention is fiercer than ever. With countless brands vying for a moment of consideration, personalized advertisements emerge not just as a strategy, but as a necessity for standing out. Understanding the role of personalized ads in the competitive digital landscape is akin to recognizing the power of calling someone by their name in a crowded room. It captures attention, builds a connection, and elevates your message above the noise.

Like a lighthouse guiding ships through treacherous waters, personalized advertising serves to direct your message to the right people at the right time. It's about illuminating the path for your target audience, making it easy for them to find what they're looking for in a sea of generic promotions. Personalization doesn't just improve the efficiency of your advertising; it enhances the consumer experience, making interactions with your brand more relevant, engaging, and memorable.

The impact of personalized advertisements goes beyond immediate engagement or conversion metrics. In the long term, it cultivates brand loyalty by demonstrating an understanding and appreciation of the consumer's unique preferences and needs. When people feel seen and heard by a brand, they're more likely to develop a sense of trust and allegiance. This emotional connection can be a powerful differentiator in a marketplace where many products and services are viewed as interchangeable.

Navigating the complexity of digital advertising requires not just a willingness to adopt new technologies but an understanding of the strategic importance of personalization. By making personalized advertising a cornerstone of your strategy, you unlock the potential to not only achieve better results but to forge deeper, more meaningful connections with your audience.

Through the lens of personalized advertising, we see the transformative power of treating your audience as individuals, not just numbers. This understanding ties together the significance of moving away from generic advertising, leveraging data and insights, and embracing

personalization in a competitive digital landscape.

Embracing Personalized Campaigns for Success

Let's recap the core essence of what we delved into in this chapter. Building **personalized, data-driven campaigns** is not just a trend; it's a necessity in today's digital landscape. By **shifting** from generic approaches to crafting **tailored campaigns**, you're acknowledging the unique needs and preferences of your audience.

Power of Audience Insights

The magic happens when you leverage **insights and data** to create ads that truly resonate with your target audience. The era of one-size-fits-all advertising is fading, giving rise to **customized messages** that speak directly to individuals, not masses.

Thriving in the Digital Jungle

Understanding the significance of **personalized ads** in the competitive online realm is the key to not just surviving but thriving. Your ability to **adapt and customize** your marketing efforts according to the intricate web of data available will set you apart from the rest.

Unlocking Profound Results

To truly excel in the digital marketing sphere, you must realize that **personalization** is not just an option; it's the secret ingredient to achieving remarkable success. By tailoring your strategies to match the **needs and desires** of your audience, you pave the way for **higher conversions** and **deeper engagement**.

In the upcoming chapters, we will delve deeper into the intricacies of **direct response advertising** in the digital age, unraveling the mysteries that surround conquering the ever-evolving landscape of online marketing.

Chapter 3: The Art of Evolution in Advertising

Amidst the hum of fluorescent lights and an orchestra of keystrokes, Molly sat in the sea of cubicles, a lone island adrift in the fathomless ocean of digital advertising. Her gaze fell upon the screen, its glow the sole beacon in her dim alcove. With each click, the marketing landscape whirled and shifted around her.

There was something akin to hunting in the way Molly approached her work, a relentless searching not for game but for patterns in data, hidden narratives in consumer behavior yet untold. She knew well the fleeting nature of relevance in her field; what worked today could easily wilt by tomorrow's relentless sun.

An email notification sliced through the mundanity, a missive from a client demanding innovation. The thought made her heart race, an imperceptible savannah where the gazelle inside her kicked against the dust. Molly realized what was at stake was not just the success of a campaign, but the survival of her own ideas in the digital ecosystem where only the fittest thrived.

Her colleagues shuffled papers and muttered meetings, but Molly was elsewhere, in a silent conference with her own doubts and resolutions. She recalled a recent trend report, the finding that short video content was king—a revelation that had her pondering late into the lonely hours. There was a quest hidden there, a quest for connections yet unseen between idea and execution, creator and consumer.

The room around her narrowed to a tunnel, her thoughts the light at its far end. She pondered over the tug of war between staying the course or embracing the unknown path, the essence of adaptation that digital advertising demanded. It was a gamble every time, for the unseen is fraught with both peril and promise. Would her conviction in the new trend be the spark that set consumer engagement ablaze?

As she stood up for a cup of coffee, her movement mere muscle memory, the warmth of the cup seeped into her fingers, a minor comfort. She considered the coffee's steadiness and how unlike it was from her daily crusade. Would her next campaign ride upon the cresting wave of change, or plummet into the trough of misjudged foresight?

Staying Ahead of the Curve: The Nonnegotiables of Digital Advertising

In the fast-paced realm of digital advertising, resting on laurels isn't just dangerous; it's commercial suicide. Continuous learning and adaptation are not merely buzzwords; they're lifelines ensuring survival and success. Every click, every ad, every campaign offers a lesson waiting to be deciphered, and the smart marketers are those who turn these insights into strategies. This conversation isn't about catching up; it's about staying ahead, remaining relevant, and driving success in an industry that waits for no one.

To excel in Meta advertising—a platform that's as dynamic as the audience it serves—requires an in-depth understanding that goes beyond the basics. Here, the key to conquest lies in not just riding the waves of change but predicting them, creating them. **Continuous learning** ensures you're always on the pulse, ready to pivot and adapt with finesse. As algorithms evolve and consumer behaviors shift like sand, staying informed and agile is your competitive edge. Thus, exploring the importance of continuous learning and adaptation isn't optional; it's foundational.

Identifying emerging trends and consumer behaviors is akin to being a digital anthropologist, observing and analyzing patterns to predict where the current will flow next. In Meta advertising, understanding these shifts can mean the difference between an overflowing funnel and a leaking bucket. It requires a keen eye, an analytical mindset, and a willingness to delve into the data with an investigative zeal. This chapter unfolds the significance of recognizing these patterns, using real-world examples to illuminate how staying attuned to digital behaviors can refine and sharpen your advertising approach.

Moreover, **continuous experimentation** is the engine of

innovation. Imagine every campaign as a hypothesis, each ad set an experiment designed to test, learn, and optimize. This relentless pursuit of improvement is what separates the good from the great, transforming average campaigns into high-performing machines. Here, we dive into practical strategies for setting up, monitoring, and iterating experiments that can significantly enhance campaign performance. Through experimentation, advertisers can discover untapped opportunities, identify cost efficiencies, and ultimately, outmaneuver competitors.

But why is all this pivotal? Because in the universe of Meta advertising, change is the only constant. Algorithms are perpetually shifting, consumer interests evolve, and what worked yesterday might not work tomorrow. Adapting strategies based on emerging trends and consumer behaviors ensures your messages resonate, engaging audiences in ways that are meaningful and impactful. This chapter serves as your compass, guiding you through the turbulent waters of digital advertising, empowering you with the knowledge to make informed, strategic decisions.

A World of Possibilities: Harnessing Insights for Impact

By engaging in continuous learning and experimentation, advertisers unlock a realm of possibilities. Each insight gleaned, every trend spotted, and each experiment conducted contributes to a richer, more effective advertising strategy. It's about transforming data into wisdom, using every click as a stepping stone towards mastery.

In the digital advertising landscape, standing still is akin to moving backwards. Thus, this chapter isn't just a collection of strategies; it's a manifesto for those ready to embrace the art of evolution in advertising. It's a call to action for marketers who aspire to not just survive but thrive, making every ad count, every campaign a lesson, and every strategy a masterpiece of adaptability and foresight. Through embracing continuous learning, identifying trends, and engaging in experimentation, the path to mastering Meta advertising becomes clear, paving the way for unparalleled success in the digital realm.

Continuous Learning: The Beacon in the Fast-Paced World of Digital Advertising

In the realm of digital advertising, the landscape shifts with the swiftness of sand in a desert storm. What worked yesterday might not hold water today, necessitating a mindset anchored in continuous learning and adaptation. This approach is not just beneficial; it's essential. The digital terrain is one marked by relentless innovation, where new platforms, tools, and consumer trends emerge at breakneck speed.

Imagine, if you will, a gardener tending to a vast and varied garden. This gardener knows that what allows one plant to thrive might cause another to wilt. Similarly, an advertiser must understand that strategies and tactics are not one-size-fits-all, and what succeeds in one campaign or platform may not in another. This metaphor underscores the importance of nurturing each campaign based on its unique needs and environment, always ready to adjust to the changing seasons of consumer interest and platform algorithms.

Every year brings forth an array of new tools and technologies designed to capture consumer attention more effectively. From evolving social media algorithms to the advent of augmented reality in ads, staying abreast of these innovations is no longer optional. It's a survival strategy. The advertisers who commit to learning and experimenting with these tools are the ones who can cut through the noise, reaching their audience more effectively.

Yet, it's not sufficient to merely stay updated. The process of adaptation involves rigorous testing and analysis. It requires a willingness to fail, learn from mistakes, and iterate swiftly. This cycle of testing, learning, and optimization is akin to evolution in the natural world—only the most adaptable and resilient thrive in changing environments.

The essence of continuous learning in digital advertising lies not just in acquiring knowledge, but in applying it creatively and strategically to stay ahead of the curve.

Keeping a Pulse on Emerging Trends and Consumer Behaviors

The digital advertising space is like a vast ocean, teeming with life and constant movement. Just as marine biologists strive to understand the behaviors of sea creatures, advertisers must delve deep into the ocean of market trends and consumer behaviors. The goal? To navigate these waters with precision, ensuring that their message reaches the intended audience.

Emerging trends and consumer behaviors are the compass by which savvy advertisers steer their strategies. For instance, the surge in mobile usage has transformed the way ads are designed and delivered. Videos are now optimized for mobile consumption, brief yet engaging, tailored to catch the eye of the scrolling user. Social media platforms introduce new features regularly, each with the potential to change the game for advertisers who are quick to adopt and experiment.

One cannot overlook the power of data analytics in this endeavor. By analyzing user engagement and behavior patterns, advertisers can gain invaluable insights into what captures interest and drives action. This data-driven approach enables a more personalized and effective advertising strategy, resonating deeply with the target audience.

Yet, recognizing trends and behaviors is only the beginning. The real challenge lies in the application—how to adapt these insights into actionable strategies that capture attention and compel action. It's a process of trial and error, of fine-tuning campaigns to align with the pulse of consumer interest.

Imagine trying to catch a fluttering butterfly in a net—the butterfly represents the ever-changing consumer interests, and the net, your advertising strategies. You must observe the butterfly's path carefully, anticipating its next move, and adjust your approach accordingly. This analogy illustrates the dynamic nature of consumer behaviors and the need for advertisers to remain flexible in their strategies.

Could recognizing and adapting to these shifts be the key to unlocking unprecedented success in your advertising efforts?

Experimentation: The Catalyst for Enhanced Campaign Performance

The call to embrace continuous experimentation in advertising echoes the spirit of innovation that marks the digital age. Experimentation is the laboratory where strategies are tested, refined, or sometimes discarded in pursuit of more effective solutions. It's the process that transforms good campaigns into great ones, pushing the boundaries of what's possible in digital advertising.

Consider the world of science for a moment—where hypotheses are formed, tested, and either validated or disproven. This scientific method is strikingly similar to the approach that forward-thinking advertisers take. They craft various versions of ads, play with different targeting options, and experiment with myriad content formats. Each campaign becomes a mini-experiment, with data collected and analyzed to determine what works best.

The beauty of experimentation lies in its capacity to surprise. Sometimes, an unexpected approach yields the most compelling results, challenging preconceived notions about what resonates with the audience. It encourages a mindset of curiosity and openness, vital traits in a landscape as varied and dynamic as digital advertising.

Moreover, experimentation provides a competitive edge. In a space where companies vie for consumer attention, the ability to innovate and adapt swiftly is a significant advantage. It means not just keeping pace but setting the pace, leading the way with creative and impactful advertising solutions.

Continuous learning, recognizing and adapting to emerging trends and consumer behaviors, and embracing experimentation are the trifecta that propels advertisers ahead in the digital realm.

Continuous Learning and Adaptation in Direct Response Advertising

Continuous learning and adaptation are not just buzzwords in the world of direct response advertising; they are the

foundation of success. In a fast-paced digital landscape where trends come and go in the blink of an eye, staying stagnant is not an option. **Embracing change** and constantly seeking new knowledge is what sets apart the average from the exceptional in this field.

Key Takeaways Reinforced

Through our exploration in this chapter, we have highlighted the **importance** of three key elements: continuous learning, identifying emerging trends, and experimentation. These pillars are not just theoretical concepts; they are **practical tools** that can elevate your advertising strategies to new heights. By absorbing new information, adapting to shifting consumer behaviors, and constantly experimenting to refine your campaigns, you are positioning yourself for success in the dynamic landscape of digital advertising.

Final Thoughts

In the ever-evolving world of digital advertising, standing still means falling behind. *Adaptation* isn't just a nice-to-have; it's a non-negotiable aspect of **success**. Be the advertiser who is always one step ahead, who anticipates rather than reacts. By harnessing the power of continuous learning and experimentation, you are not only keeping pace with the competition; you are setting the pace. Let curiosity be your compass, and let innovation be your guide as you navigate the exciting terrain of direct response advertising.

Chapter 4: Balancing Creativity with Analytics

The sun shot glares through the crisp autumn window of the downtown agency where Samantha stood, face reflected in the looming computer screen. Her fingers danced a hesitant waltz over the keyboard. The client needed a campaign – a bridge of stories that would sweep the consumers from the towers of uncertainty into the assured haven of their brand. The clock on the wall ticked in rhythm with Samantha's own heart, each second a reminder that these ads were not just a job, but a test of her ability to marry numbers and narratives.

Her thoughts drifted to the briefing session. "Creative storytelling is paramount," the client had proclaimed, their eyes alive with the fire of someone who believes in the power of myth. But Samantha knew that this fervor needed a backbone of data to stand erect. She pressed a palm against her forehead, the coolness of her skin a stark contrast to the warmth cascading through the office. Was she an artist or an analyst? Yet the question was misleading, for neither could exist in the vacuum of the other's absence.

She recalled the campaigns of her past, ones that fizzled out despite their ornate tapestries of fiction because they lacked the rigidity of analytics. The lesson had been hard-taught; she understood the interplay between the two now. The crisp air snuck in through the marginally ajar window, the city below breathed a life of transactions and transitions.

Reaching out, she flipped through the pages of data laid bare before her. Click-through rates, conversion percentages, demographic breakdowns. These were not just numbers, they were the pulsing desires and aversions of a thousand nameless faces. She breathed life into these figures, sculpting them into a narrative that could speak, that could feel.

A sudden burst of laughter from across the room drew her attention for a split second - the real world vying for her presence. She smiled faintly, reminded that beyond these campaigns were people, not just consumers but individuals seeking connections, affirmation, stories to which they could anchor their dreams. It was this humanity that she sought to capture, dress in the finery of datasets and project upon the stage of the client's needs.

What if she could craft a tale so seamless, woven with the golden threads of data, that it could indeed drive a man to love a brand as one might cherish a well-worn book or whisper of a memory? Would it then be possible, Samantha wondered, to make the heart loyal not through the force of habit, but through the gentle pull of a story well told?

Unleashing the Fusion of Art and Science in Your Advertising Campaigns

In an era where digital advertising has become more sophisticated and competitive, mastering the craft of creating effective ads on Meta platforms demands a fine balance between creativity and analytics. The journey to direct response success is not solely driven by artistic whims or cold, hard data; it is the seamless integration of these two realms that elevates campaigns from purely transactional to genuinely transformative experiences for audiences. Understanding this dichotomy and learning how to harness its power is crucial for anyone looking to outwit algorithms, outmaneuver competitors, and outperform expectations.

At the heart of every successful Meta ad campaign lies the synergy of **data-driven decision-making and creative storytelling**. These are not opposing forces; rather, they complement each other, providing advertisers with a comprehensive toolkit to engage, persuade, and convert their target audience. To navigate this complex landscape, one must first recognize the necessity of embracing analytics as the foundation for decision-making. This serves as the compass, guiding advertisers through the vast sea of metrics to pinpoint what truly resonates with their audience.

However, leveraging data is only half the battle. The art of **crafting compelling narratives** that connect on a human level cannot be overlooked. This is where your brand's unique voice and vision come into play, transforming raw numbers into memorable stories that leave a lasting impression. By infusing your ads with creativity that speaks to your audience's aspirations, challenges, and desires, you create an emotional bridge that analytics alone cannot build.

The magic happens when optimization techniques and engaging narratives join forces. Imagine your campaign as a finely tuned orchestra, where data insights act as the conductor, guiding the creative elements to perform in harmony. This approach allows for the continuous refinement of your ads, ensuring they not only capture attention but also drive meaningful action. *Remember, an ad that resonates on an emotional level but fails to convert is a missed opportunity, just as an optimized ad that lacks soul will struggle to leave a mark.*

In this pursuit, the ultimate goal is to create campaigns that not only drive conversions but also foster brand loyalty and engagement. This is achieved by delivering value at every touchpoint, making each interaction with your brand an enriching experience. Your ability to blend analytical precision with creative flair will set you apart in a crowded digital landscape, turning viewers into advocates and clicks into loyal customers.

Strategies for Masterful Integration

So, how do you achieve this delicate balance? Start by adopting a test-and-learn mentality, treating each campaign as an experiment where data informs creative adjustments. Pay close attention to the performance indicators that matter most to your brand's objectives, and let these insights shape your storytelling efforts. Also, don't shy away from leveraging the latest ad technologies and formats to present your narratives in the most engaging way possible. Always keep your audience at the center of your strategy, adapting your message to meet their evolving needs and preferences.

Above all, remember that mastering the art of balancing creativity with analytics is a journey, not a destination. The digital advertising landscape is ever-changing, with new platforms, tools, and consumer behaviors emerging all the time. Staying curious, flexible, and committed to learning will not only enhance your Meta ad mastery but also ensure that your campaigns continue to resonate in an increasingly complex and competitive environment.

By embracing this holistic approach to advertising, you'll find that the path to direct response success on Meta is both an art and a science. It's a dynamic process that demands continuous experimentation, evaluation, and iteration. Armed with the insights from this chapter, you're now better equipped to navigate this terrain, crafting campaigns that expertly balance data-driven optimization with the power of creative storytelling.

Understanding the critical nature of fusing data-driven decision-making with creative storytelling is paramount in the dynamic realm of Meta advertising. In the digital age, where data is abundant, advertisers have the tools to tailor their campaigns with unprecedented precision. Yet, this abundance of data also presents a challenge. Without the infusion of creativity, campaigns risk becoming lost in a sea of noise, failing to capture the attention or imagination of the intended audience.

Think of the digital advertising space as a garden. Data is like the soil, rich in nutrients and potential, but without the seeds of creativity, nothing will grow. Analytics provide insights into the nature of the soil and the conditions of the environment. However, it is the storyteller who plants the seeds, deciding not just what will grow, but how it will be nurtured to capture the beauty and interest of those who wander through.

On the flip side, creative narratives without the support of data-driven optimization risk missing the mark. They may tell a compelling story, but if they're not reaching the right audience, at the right time, and through the right channels, their impact is diminished. It's akin to planting a beautiful flower in the shade when it needs full sun to thrive. The beauty of the story is lost if it can't find its audience.

Integrating these two facets allows for a symbiotic relationship where each element enhances the other. Data informs the creative process, identifying not just who the audience is but what they care about, how they speak, and where they spend their time. In turn, creativity breathes life into these insights, crafting stories that resonate on a personal level, compelling engagement and action. This is not a one-time process but a cycle of constant refinement and optimization. It demands a willingness to learn from each campaign, using data to iterate and enhance the creative narrative over time.

In essence, the marriage of data-driven decision-making with compelling storytelling is not just beneficial—it's essential for advertisers aiming to thrive in the vibrant, ever-evolving landscape of Meta advertising.

Discover How to Combine Optimization Techniques with Engaging Narratives for Compelling Ads

Merging optimization techniques with engaging narratives is akin to conducting a symphony where each note and instrument plays its part in harmony. Optimization provides the tempo and the rhythm, setting the pace for how and when the narrative unfolds across different channels and moments. Engaging narratives, on the other hand, provide the melody, the memorable piece that captures hearts and minds.

To achieve this harmony, one must first understand the tools at their disposal. Meta's advertising platforms offer a suite of analytical tools designed to measure and refine campaign performance across a myriad of metrics. Click-through rates, engagement metrics, conversion rates, and more, all serve as indicators of an ad's resonance with its intended audience.

Yet, data without interpretation is just numbers. It requires a discerning eye to extract actionable insights from this wealth of information. For instance, higher engagement rates on a video ad could signal the story's appeal, but pairing this data with time spent watching the ad might reveal whether the message is fully consumed or if adjustments are necessary.

This is where storytelling enters the stage, crafting narratives that not only captivate but are tailored to resonate based on the insights garnered. The art lies in weaving these narratives in a way that feels personal and engaging to the audience, yet flexible enough to adapt based on performance data. A/B testing becomes your rehearsal, allowing you to fine-tune the narrative, imagery, and call to actions based on direct feedback from your audience.

Imagine a story that changes course in response to the listener's reactions, adjusting its pace, tone, and details to keep them engaged. This is the potential of combining optimization techniques with engaging narratives. Through this dance of data and creativity, ads become more than just messages; they become experiences that resonate and compel action.

What if the secret to captivating your audience lies not just in telling a better story or in optimizing your ads, but in the seamless integration of both?

Learning to Create Campaigns that Drive Conversions and Foster Brand Loyalty

Creating campaigns that not only drive conversions but also foster brand loyalty and engagement is the pinnacle of advertising success. This achievement is not merely about making a sale; it's about initiating a relationship with the customer, one that is built on trust and continued engagement.

Consider a favorite local café that remembers your order or a clothing brand that knows your style so well, it feels like they craft each piece just for you. This blend of personalization and engagement creates a sense of loyalty and affection for the brand. Now, imagine translating this feeling into your digital campaigns. This is the essence of creating ads that not only convert but also build relationships.

Data analytics lays the groundwork for understanding your audience's preferences, behaviors, and pain points. This knowledge allows advertisers to tailor their messaging and offers to match specific customer needs and desires. However, personalization is just the first step. The next phase involves crafting a narrative that speaks directly to the audience, connecting on an emotional level. It's about telling a story that resonates, reflects their experiences, or inspires them, making your brand a part of their personal story.

Moreover, fostering brand loyalty is about consistency over time. It's about delivering on promises and maintaining the quality of interaction across all touchpoints, from ads to customer service. Each campaign should feel like a chapter in a larger story, where the audience eagerly anticipates what comes next, knowing they'll be met with the same level of personal attention and care.

This strategy goes beyond a single purchase. It builds a community of loyal followers who are not just customers but advocates for your brand. They are the individuals who will champion your products or services to friends and family, making the ultimate conversion from customer to brand ambassador.

Integrating data-driven strategies with creative storytelling, optimizing narratives based on analytics, and consistently delivering engaging content form the triad that underpins campaigns capable of driving conversions while simultaneously fostering brand loyalty and engagement.

The Power of Balance

Balancing data and creativity is the secret sauce to exceptional ad performance. It's not enough to just have one or the other; **integrating analytical insights with captivating narratives** is where the magic truly happens. By **combining data-driven optimization with engaging storytelling**, you're creating a potent formula for success in the world of advertising on Meta platforms.

A Winning Combination

Data-driven decision-making helps you understand your audience and their behavior, guiding you on where to focus your efforts. On the other hand, **creative storytelling** brings your brand to life, captivating your audience and fostering emotional connections. The synergy of these two elements is where campaigns truly shine, driving both **conversions and long-term loyalty**.

Elevating Your Strategy

As you move forward in your advertising endeavors, remember that **balancing analytics with creativity** is not a one-time task but an ongoing process. Continuously refine your strategy, test new ideas, and stay open to innovative approaches. By embracing this **holistic approach**, you position yourself for success in the ever-evolving landscape of digital advertising.

Embrace the Journey

The journey of mastering the art of **balancing creativity with analytics** is not just about achieving short-term wins but about building a sustainable, impactful strategy for the long haul. As you strive for excellence in your advertising efforts, remember that the true essence of success lies in finding the delicate equilibrium between the art and science of advertising.

Takeaways for Success

Now that you've delved into the intricacies of merging data-driven insights with compelling storytelling, remember that the true power lies in **harmonizing these elements**. Keep refining your approach, experimenting with new ideas, and always striving to strike that perfect balance in your campaigns. By mastering this blend, you'll be well on your way to conquering the realm of digital advertising on Meta platforms.

Chapter 5: Mastering the Targeting Battlefield

Jordan's fingertips dance across the keyboard in the dim light of a cramped, upstairs office. This room, cluttered with books and papers, smells of stale coffee and worn leather. A singular window, obscured by drapes heavy with dust, mutes the bustle of the world outside. The radiant glow of twin computer screens casts shadows across his face in the otherwise darkened space.

Today, the gravity of his task sinks deep – to chart a course through the digital expanse, to discover that fabled intersection of right person and right moment. He's an architect of attention, designing campaigns that whisper directly into the hearts of those scrolling by. His canvas pulses with the traffic of a billion thoughts, hopes, and desires orchestrated by the Meta platforms' engines.

A soft chime interrupts the stillness around him. It's a message from Mia, his colleague, reminding him of the weight their work carries. They are the hidden navigators of the digital seas, unseen yet pivotal, steering businesses toward the shores of profitability. And Jordan, with every keystroke, sculpts the currents.

His musing breaks with a sigh. He remembers campaigns

past, how some soared high on the wings of precision while others fell, grounded by the mistiming of intentions and actions. He recalls a particular ad, art and copy harmonized like a symphony, yet it played to an empty hall, the audience elsewhere. Each success, each misstep, a lesson etched into his tactics.

The clock on the wall ticks relentlessly. Time, he muses, is the elusive factor in the equation of conversion. How can he predict the instance when a scrolling finger pauses, the heartbeat when a decision turns from casual interest to firm conviction? His gaze returns to the screen where data points transform into insights, pulling back the curtain on behavior, revealing patterns in the labyrinth of human interaction.

In his quest for that perfect segment, that ideal time, there emerges a narrative from beyond the screen. It weaves through the analytics, a tale of connections made and missed, of messages resonating in harmony with the rhythms of daily existence.

Why do some resonate while others are lost in the noise? This question lingers in the stale air, an invitation to journey deeper into the realm of human connection.

Navigating the minefield of digital advertising requires more than just throwing your message into the virtual world and hoping for the best. It demands precision, strategy, and an in-depth understanding of who you're speaking to. Now, imagine turning this battlefield into your playground, where every move is calculated, and your ads are sharpshooters, hitting the bullseye of your target market. That's the essence of mastering advanced targeting strategies on Meta platforms. You're not just reaching out to people; you're connecting with the right ones at the perfect moment, maximally boosting your ad performance and conversion rates.

Craft Your Sniper Scope: Pinpointing Your Audience

Let's dive into the heart of advanced targeting strategies, starting with **defining your target audience**. A crucial first step, yet often glossed over for its simplicity. But here's where it gets interesting. Imagine having a bird's eye view of your battlefield, where every potential customer is a moving target. By identifying specifics of demographics, interests, and behaviors, you're essentially crafting a sniper scope, zeroing in on your targets with precision. This isn't about broad strokes; it's about chiseling down to the fine details that make your audience unique.

Next is leveraging the power of **audience insights** provided by Meta. Think of it as gathering intelligence on the enemy terrain. You're not flying blind; you're using gathered data to sharpen your aim, refining your targeting strategy to ensure your campaigns strike chords with the right segments. This isn't just a guesswork game; it's a strategic move grounded in data.

Building Your Arsenal: Custom and Lookalike Audiences

As we delve deeper, we explore the weaponry at your disposal — **custom and lookalike audiences**. Custom audiences allow you to retarget people who have already shown an interest in your brand, whether through your website, app, or social media pages. It's like having inside information on who's already curious about your offerings, making it easier to tailor your messaging. On the other side, lookalike audiences extend this reach, enabling you to clone your best customers. It's like training your sniper scope on doppelgangers of your existing fan base, expanding your territory in the most efficient way possible.

Interest and behavioral targeting follow suit as potent tools in your arsenal. **Interest targeting** zeroes in on individuals based on their declared interests on the Meta platform. It's akin to tuning into their conversations and understanding what makes them tick. Simultaneously, **behavioral targeting** focuses on their actions — what they purchase, the content they engage with, making your targeting strategy dynamic and responsive to real-world behaviors.

The Art of War: Combining Forces

However, the true art lies in the combination of these

strategies. Just as a general wouldn't rely on a single type of unit to win a battle, **combining targeting options** creates a formidable force. This multidimensional approach ensures your ads resonate on a deeper level, reaching a well-defined audience ready to engage and convert.

Sharpening the Blade: Continuous Improvement

Lastly, **monitoring and analyzing performance** isn't just a cleanup operation; it's an integral part of your strategy. Every ad campaign response is a treasure trove of insights, helping refine and perfect your targeting efforts. This cycle of deployment, analysis, and adjustment is what keeps your strategy razor-sharp, always ready for the changing dynamics of the digital battlefield.

Target Acquired: Navigating Meta's Terrain

Mastering advanced targeting strategies on Meta platforms is akin to being the grandmaster in a high-stakes game of chess. Every move is deliberate, every strategy finely tuned to ensure your message not only reaches but resonates with the right audience. By following this meticulously laid out process, you're not just sending out ads; you're deploying targeted missives designed to convert, engage, and ultimately triumph in the competitive landscape of digital advertising. With every step, you're not just aiming; you're hitting the mark, turning prospects into loyalists—one targeted ad at a time.

Grasping Advanced Targeting Strategies

In the realm of direct response advertising, understanding how to zero in on specific audience segments is akin to becoming an expert marksman. Each ad you deploy is an arrow, and your targeting strategy determines the precision with which it hits the bullseye. Advanced targeting strategies allow advertisers to sift through the vast digital landscape, identifying and engaging with their ideal audience segments. This level of precision not only conserves resources but also maximizes the impact of each advertising effort.

Imagine you're at a bustling market, surrounded by stalls upon stalls of vibrant goods and chattering crowds. Each stallholder uses signs, shouts, and showcases to attract customers. However, the ones who understand their customers' specific needs and preferences can draw them in more effectively, even in such a chaotic atmosphere. They've mastered the art of targeting. Similarly, the digital marketplace is flooded with content, making it crucial to employ advanced targeting strategies to ensure your messages reach the right eyes and ears among the multitude.

To achieve this, advertisers must delve deep into their audience's demographics, interests, and behaviors. This involves collecting and analyzing data from a variety of sources, including website analytics, social media interactions, and previous ad performances. By weaving together these threads of information, advertisers can form a detailed tapestry of their target audience. This refined understanding enables them to tailor their messaging and ad placements precisely, ensuring that each campaign resonates deeply with its intended recipients.

However, it's not enough to simply identify and target specific audience segments. Advertisers must continuously refine and adapt their strategies based on performance data and changing audience behaviors. This dynamic approach allows for the agile optimization of campaigns, ensuring that they remain effective over time. Just as a chef tastes and adjusts their dishes throughout the cooking process, advertisers must tweak their targeting strategies, keeping them fresh and impactful.

Mastering advanced targeting strategies equips advertisers to launch campaigns that hit the mark every time, maximizing both reach and resonance with their selected audience segments.

Advanced Targeting Strategies for Pinpointing Specific Audience Segments

Step 1: Define Your Target Audience

The foundation of any successful advertising campaign lies in a clear understanding of who you're trying to reach. This goes beyond basic demographics to encompass interests, behaviors, and even nuances in preferences. It's about painting a comprehensive picture of your ideal customer — creating a sharp, detailed snapshot rather than a blurred, generalized image.

Step 2: Utilize Audience Insights

Audience insights are like a treasure trove of information, unlocking the secrets to what makes your target audience tick. Here, the Meta platform plays a crucial role, offering a deep dive into the data that sheds light on the preferences and behaviors of your audience. This knowledge is pivotal in honing your targeting to surgical precision.

Step 3: Utilize Custom Audiences

Imagine you have a list of people who already have shown interest in what you're offering. By creating custom audiences, you're essentially inviting these individuals back for a closer look, using their past interactions to guide the conversation. This approach adds a layer of intimacy and relevance to your ads, significantly enhancing their effectiveness.

Step 4: Explore Lookalike Audiences

Building lookalike audiences is like cloning your best customers, but without the ethical quandaries. By identifying the common traits among your current audience, Meta helps you cast a wider net to find new people who share similar characteristics. This expands your reach without diluting the relevance of your targeting.

Step 5: Implement Interest Targeting

Interest targeting allows you to tap into the passions and preferences that make each user on the Meta platform unique. By aligning your ads with these interests, you're effectively inserting your message into the ongoing conversation happening in their minds, increasing the chances of engagement and action.

Step 6: Utilize Behavioral Targeting

Understanding user behavior online offers invaluable insights into how to tailor your advertising. Behavioral targeting takes advantage of patterns in engagement, purchase history, and ad interaction to predict future interests and intent. It's about predicting need before it's directly expressed, placing your ad right where it needs to be.

Step 7: Combine Targeting Options

The real magic happens when you blend multiple targeting techniques, layering them to create a complex, multidimensional strategy. This approach allows for nuanced targeting, hitting different audience segments in the most impactful way possible. Think of it as crafting a multifaceted narrative, with each technique adding depth and texture to your campaign story.

Step 8: Monitor and Analyze Targeting Performance

Last but not least, the cycle of refinement is perpetual. Monitoring, analyzing, and tweaking your targeting approach based on performance data is critical for sustained success. It's a loop of learning and adapting, where each iteration hones the precision of your targeting mechanisms.

How can refining and combining these targeting strategies further amplify the effectiveness of your campaigns?

Navigating the Complexities of Meta Platforms' Targeting

Imagine navigating an intricate web, where each strand represents a different characteristic, interest, or behavior of the vast user base on Meta platforms. Successfully maneuvering through this web requires an understanding that goes beyond the surface, delving deep into the intricacies of audience behavior and platform capabilities. This is where the complexity of Meta's targeting system reveals itself.

To effectively navigate this complexity, advertisers must start by dissecting their audience into manageable segments. This is similar to separating puzzle pieces based on color or pattern before beginning to assemble the picture. By identifying and categorizing audience demographics, interests, and behaviors, advertisers can lay the groundwork for precise targeting strategies that resonate with each unique segment.

Feedback Loops and Iterative Testing

A critical component of mastering Meta's targeting capabilities is the incorporation of feedback loops. Imagine setting a course for a ship based on the stars, then adjusting as the sea and wind alter its path. Similarly, advertisers must continuously adapt their targeting strategies based on performance data. These feedback loops ensure that campaigns are optimized in real-time, with each adjustment bringing the advertiser closer to their desired outcome.

Incorporating External Factors

In the rapidly evolving digital advertising landscape, external factors such as privacy regulations and shifts in social media usage trends can significantly impact targeting effectiveness. Navigating these changes requires a proactive approach, where advertisers anticipate and adjust to external influences just as a navigator alters course in anticipation of an approaching storm.

Decision Nodes and Campaign Objectives

Within this complex system, decision nodes serve as critical junctions where advertisers must choose the path that aligns best with their campaign objectives. Whether the goal is brand awareness, lead generation, or direct sales, each decision point guides the advertiser towards the targeting options that promise the greatest impact.

The Importance of Adaptation

Ultimately, the key to mastering Meta's targeting capabilities lies in the ability to adapt. This involves not just a set-and-forget approach, but an ongoing commitment to refining and evolving targeting strategies. By embracing flexibility and a willingness to experiment, advertisers can stay ahead of the curve, ensuring their campaigns continue to engage and convert even as the digital landscape shifts.

In mastering advanced targeting strategies, ensuring ads reach the right audience at the ideal time, and navigating the complexities of Meta platforms' targeting, advertisers can significantly boost the likelihood of conversion, transforming targeting from a challenge into a competitive advantage.

Elevating Your Direct Response Advertising

Success

Mastering advanced targeting strategies is **fundamental** for driving successful direct response advertising campaigns on Meta platforms. By grasping advanced targeting techniques to pinpoint specific audience segments based on demographics, interests, and behaviors, advertisers can **maximize** ad performance and boost conversion likelihood. It's essential to ensure that your ads reach the right audience at the ideal time to make the most significant impact.

Understanding the complexities of Meta platforms' targeting options is **crucial**. By navigating these complexities effectively, advertisers can unlock the potential to outwit algorithms, outmaneuver competitors, and ultimately outperform expectations. Advertisers who take the time to hone in on advanced targeting strategies will undoubtedly see a significant improvement in their ad campaigns' success rates.

Take the Next Step

As you continue on your journey to conquer the digital advertising landscape, remember that **mastery** of targeting is an ongoing process. Keep testing, refining, and adapting your strategies to stay ahead of the game. The knowledge and insights gained from this chapter will set the foundation for your future success in direct response advertising.

Continue to refine your targeting strategies, experiment

with different audience segments, and stay up to date with the latest trends and features. Your dedication to mastering the targeting battlefield will pay off in the form of increased conversions, higher ad performance, and a competitive edge in the digital advertising arena.

In the next chapter, we will delve into the art of crafting compelling ad creatives that resonate with your target audience and drive action. Get ready to elevate your ad game even further and learn how to create ads that capture attention and inspire clicks.

Chapter 6: Creative Mastery for Audience Engagement

The morning sun peeked through the slats of the Venetian blinds, casting long, striped shadows across the room. Alex sat huddled at a timeworn desk that bore the marks of countless coffee cups and the occasional, reckless swing of a pen cap. Amidst the clutter of papers, a weather-beaten laptop displayed a collage of vibrant images and half-written slogans. There was an impending sense of urgency—of missing pieces waiting to be discovered in the cacophony of color and text.

The clock on the wall ticked with a rhythm that seemed too methodical, too indifferent to the chaos of creation. Alex felt each minute and each second pressed upon their shoulders, as if time itself had taken a personal interest in reminding them of deadlines and expectations. Invested in the task, there was a pursuit for the perfect blend of form and function within the artifacts of advertising—a pursuit for the holy grail of design that could capture attention and prompt action.

A fresh aroma of ground coffee wafted in from the nearby café, luring the senses, offering a brief respite from the labor of creativity. Alex considered a break, a brief surrender, but the thought was fleeting. The images on the laptop called louder, a siren song of unfinished business. Each element in the ads Alex crafted was more than mere decoration; they were the silent ambassadors of brand identity, the shepherds guiding a flock of impulses towards conversion.

There was the recollection of a campaign that had soared, where each creative choice had seemed touched by serendipity. And yet, the ghost of a campaign past that had faltered lingered, a specter woven from good intentions but poor execution. These memories danced in and out of consciousness, a reminder that the line between success and failure was as thin as the blade of creativity.

Interruptions came in the form of distant laughter from the street below, the flutter of pigeons taking flight, the sudden chill as a cloud veiled the sun's warmth. Alex acknowledged them without passion, their existence merely accents in the symphony of a mind at work. The focus remained unyielded, trained on aligning the elemental with the complex—imagery with message, aesthetic with strategy—on crafting ad creatives that not merely existed but lived, breathed, persuaded.

Will the ads that emerge from the clutter of this desk forge connections, inspire action, and etch themselves into the fabric of the viewer's day? Or will they dissolve into the white noise of digital existence, unseen, unheard, unfelt?

In the bustling digital marketplace, standing out is more challenging than ever. Yet, it's not impossible. It necessitates merging art and strategy to craft ad creatives that don't just capture attention but hold it, compelling the audience to act. This bridge between engagement and action is where the magic happens, and it's exactly what this section of our journey is about. Dive deep into the core of what makes ad creatives on Meta platforms - Facebook, Instagram, WhatsApp, and Messenger - not just seen, but effective. Let's explore how creativity marries strategy to elevate your Meta ad campaigns from merely existing to performing.

The Power of First Impressions

The digital world is a crowded place. Your ad has a split second to make an impression. But how? First, understand that **the visual elements of your ad are the frontline soldiers in the battle for attention**. A compelling image or video can stop a potential customer in their tracks, but it's the harmony of message and visuals that keep them engaged. Here you'll learn the delicate art of blending visuals with a clear, compelling message that resonates with your audience, making them feel seen and understood.

Emotion Drives Action

It's been said that people buy emotions, not products. This principle holds its ground firmly in the realm of digital advertising. *Understanding the emotional journey* you want your audience to take is crucial. Whether it's the joy of discovery, the thrill of an offer, or the relief of finding a solution, crafting your ad around these emotional touchpoints can dramatically increase the likelihood of conversion. But it's not just about the what; it's the how. Show don't tell how your product fits into their lives, not just why it's better than the competition.

The Art and Science of Conversion

Did you know that specific creative elements can significantly enhance your conversion rates? From the color scheme and imagery to the call-to-action (CTA), each element plays a pivotal role. For instance, certain colors can evoke specific emotions, influencing how your brand is perceived. Likewise, a powerful CTA does more than prompt action; it offers a clear path forward. By understanding the psychology behind these elements, **you can optimize your ad creatives for maximum impact**, steering viewers towards the desired action.

Best Practices for a Winning Strategy

In the pursuit of crafting irresistible ad creatives, there's a treasure trove of best practices to be unearthed. These include leveraging user-generated content for authenticity, using A/B testing to understand what resonates with your audience, and ensuring your creatives are optimized for every device and platform. **Alignment with your brand's voice and identity** is non-negotiable, ensuring every creative piece not only grabs attention but also builds on the cohesive image of your brand.

In navigating the crowded waters of Meta platforms, remember the role of innovative, engaging creatives in connecting with your audience on a deeper level. They're not just looking to be sold to; they're looking for experiences that resonate, solutions that excite them, and brands they can relate to and trust. By mastering the principles of designing captivating ad creatives, understanding the role these creatives play in driving conversions and brand awareness, and adhering to best practices, you equip yourself with the tools to not just exist but excel in the digital arena.

Keep these insights as your compass as you forge ahead, blending creativity with strategy, art with science, to create ad campaigns that don't just aim for clicks but strive for engagement, building lasting relationships with your audience. This isn't just about standing out; it's about being remembered, creating an indelible mark in the minds and hearts of your audience. Embrace the creative journey, and watch as your Meta ad campaigns transform from mere noise in the digital expanse to symphonies of engagement and conversion.

Principles of Designing Attention-Capturing Ad Creatives

In the bustling digital marketplace, standing out is not just an option; it's a necessity. The first principle of designing ad creatives that capture attention and prompt action is clarity. A clear message, uncluttered visuals, and a straightforward call-to-action (CTA) ensure that the audience understands what you're offering and what step they should take next. It's akin to being the beacon of light in a foggy harbor, guiding ships safely to port.

Following clarity, relevance plays a crucial role. Your creative should resonate with your target audience's interests, needs, and desires. This alignment can be thought of as finding the right key for a lock. Every audience segment has a unique 'lock,' and your creative must be the 'key' that fits perfectly, unlocking their engagement and interest.

Visual hierarchy guides the viewer's eye through your ad, emphasizing the most crucial elements first. This can be achieved through the use of size, color, and spatial positioning. Imagine a well-organized shelf where the most necessary items are within easy reach and prominently displayed. Similarly, your ad should arrange elements in a way that naturally draws the eye to what's most important.

Consistency across your branding and messaging reinforces recognition and trust. Like a familiar voice in a crowded room, your ad should stand out to your audience because it speaks in a tone and style they've come to recognize and trust. This doesn't mean every ad has to look the same, but there should be a familial resemblance that cues the audience into who is speaking.

The golden rule is designing with the audience in mind, ensuring clarity, relevance, visual hierarchy, and consistency to captivate attention and encourage action.

The Power of Creative Elements in Conversion and Brand Awareness

Creative elements are the building blocks of any memorable ad. They combine to tell a story that not only entertains but also educates and persuades. The role they play in driving conversions and building brand awareness cannot be overstated. Just like spices in a dish, the right combination can elevate your ad from good to unforgettable, leaving a lasting impression on the consumer's mind.

First, visuals grab attention. Bright colors, dynamic images, and engaging video content act as the initial handshake between your brand and the audience. It's that first glance across the room that says, "There's something interesting here." But it's the substance behind the style - the message that these visuals convey - that moves an audience from interest to action.

Copywriting, then, is the voice of your brand. The right words can inspire, challenge, and reassure. Effective copy doesn't just talk to an audience; it speaks to them. It's like having a conversation with a good friend – it flows, feels natural, and, most importantly, it's genuine. It's in this authenticity that a brand finds its groove and resonates with its audience on a deeper level.

Calls-to-action (CTAs) are your closer. No ad is complete without a clear, compelling CTA that guides the audience toward the next step. This could be anything from signing up for a newsletter to making a purchase. Think of CTAs as the map that shows the treasure hunters where X marks the spot. Without it, they're intrigued but ultimately lost on what to do next.

Emotion drives action. Whether it's humor, empathy, excitement, or urgency, emotional appeal creates a deeper connection with the audience. It's the difference between hearing a song that's technically impressive and one that makes you feel something. The latter sticks with you, replaying in your mind long after the first listen.

Integration across platforms ensures consistency in your message, no matter where your audience encounters your brand. In a world where consumers are bombarded by information, being unmistakable in your identity across platforms is like a lighthouse beacon guiding ships through the night. It offers a point of reference that's both reassuring and guiding.

How can you mix the right creative ingredients to not only catch the eye but also capture the heart and lead to decisive action?

Best Practices for Crafting Effective Ad Creatives on Meta Platforms

Crafting ad creatives that resonate and perform well on Meta platforms demands a strategy that aligns with both the platform's capabilities and the audience's preferences. The first step in this process is understanding the unique environment of Meta's platforms, where visual content reigns supreme. This is visual storytelling, where your brand's narrative unfolds in the frame of a smartphone screen.

The use of high-quality visuals cannot be understated. In the scroll of a feed, your ad has a fleeting moment to make an impact. Think of it as a billboard on a high-speed highway; it needs to be bold, clear, and compelling enough to be understood at a glance. A sharp image or a captivating video can be the difference between a scroll-past and a stop-and-engage.

Customization for the audience segment and platform is key. Each platform under the Meta umbrella has its own culture and language. Crafting your message to fit these nuances is like changing your attire to suit the occasion – it shows respect and understanding for the audience and the environment you're engaging with.

Testing and optimization cannot be overlooked. What worked yesterday might not work tomorrow, and the only way to stay ahead is to continually test different elements of your creative, from imagery to ad copy to CTA placement. This is the scientific method applied to marketing – hypothesize, test, analyze, and adapt.

Finally, leveraging platform-specific features such as interactive elements, augmented reality, and shopping capabilities can significantly enhance engagement and conversion rates. Using these tools effectively is akin to adding a new dimension to your storytelling, inviting the audience not just to view but to participate in the tale you're weaving.

Understanding the environment, choosing high-quality visuals, customizing for the audience and platform, continuously testing, and leveraging unique features are the cornerstones of crafting ad creatives that enhance campaign effectiveness on Meta platforms.

Elevating Your Creative Mastery

Crafting ad creatives that speak directly to your audience is not just an art; it's a science. **Capturing attention, evoking emotion, and prompting action** are the magic ingredients that transform a simple ad into a powerful tool for engagement and conversion.

Unleashing the Power of Creative Elements

In the competitive landscape of digital marketing, **creative elements are the heart of your ad strategy**. They are the visual and textual cues that tell your brand's story, build awareness, and ultimately drive conversions. Don't underestimate their impact—they are the secret weapon you need to win over your audience.

Mastering the Art of Crafting Compelling Ads

By following **best practices for ad creatives**, you're not just creating visuals and copy—you're creating an experience that resonates with your audience. **Every color choice, every word, every image matters**. It's your chance to leave a lasting impression and make a meaningful connection with those who encounter your ad on Meta platforms.

Remember, the world of digital advertising is constantly evolving. Stay agile, be bold, and never stop refining your creative approach. In the next chapter, we'll delve into the strategic side of campaign optimization, so get ready to take your Meta ad game to the next level.

Chapter 7: Optimization Techniques for Peak Performance

Early morning light crept through the venetian blinds, casting striped shadows across the cluttered desk where Jordan sat, surrounded by the humming of computers and the faint scent of stale air. He had become a monument to the digital age, his hands nearly fused to the keyboard from the ceaseless clacking. In each click and tap, lay his search for answers to the labyrinth of user engagement and conversion rates that had plagued his recent online campaigns.

Jordan's focus flitted from graphs to charts, his brain working through patterns like a mathematician divining secrets from numbers. But the conversions, the all-important validations of his efforts, were as elusive as a pleasant memory in a mind riddled with doubts. He remembered the days when results seemed to manifest from sheer will, but now each metric felt stubborn, unyielding.

He leaned close to the screen, eyes narrowing at the bounce rates and the abandoned shopping carts that unfolded before him. It was as if users were brushing by his calls-to-action and landing pages like strangers at a bus stop, acknowledging their existence only with a glance before moving on. He could almost hear their collective thoughts dissipating into cyberspace, uncaptured and unconverted.

The silent companionship of the room was broken by the ring of his phone. It was a call from his boss, a reminder that the churning sea of data, of lost opportunities and soaring bounce rates, was not his alone to navigate. They spoke of expectations and targets, words that hovered like clouds ready to burst. As he hung up, the weight of the conversation anchored itself to his shoulders.

He rose and paced the narrow confines of the office, stepping over a power cord snaking its way to a surge protector. The physical movement provided a momentary respite from the digital world where his challenges lay in wait. For a moment he stood there, letting the morning light wash over him, trying to remember a time when solutions were not barricaded behind screens and code.

Out there in the sunlit world, every door handle, every handshake was a call-to-action, and the successful conversions were the laughs shared, the relationships formed. Could it be that within the sterile digital landscape he'd forgotten the very human element that once guided his intuition?

As the day ticked onwards, and Jordan returned to his digital domain, the fundamentals lingered in his mind. He realized that understanding the dance of human interaction was still at the heart of it all. Could it be that real engagement was less about algorithms and more about the fundamental desires connecting people everywhere?

But how does one translate the warmth of human connection into the pixels and clicks of an online world?

Unlocking the Art of Meta Ad Optimization: Your Blueprint to Amplified Conversions

In the fast-evolving world of digital advertising, standing out and making a genuine impact can feel like trying to solve a complex puzzle blindfolded. The key, however, lies in mastering the nuances of optimization—particularly on platforms like Meta, where the competition is fierce, and the algorithms ever-changing. This journey into optimization isn't just about tweaking a few settings here and there; it's about strategizing, testing, and fine-tuning every aspect of your ads and landing pages to reach peak performance. It's an ongoing process of learning, adapting, and outsmarting the competition to not just meet but exceed your campaign objectives.

The focal point of this journey is threefold: **enhancing user experience, refining key campaign elements, and unlocking the potential for higher conversion rates**. Let's delve into why these aspects are non-negotiable in the pursuit of digital advertising success. First and foremost, the digital space is user-centric. If your campaigns and landing pages aren't tailored to offer a seamless, engaging user experience, chances are you'll lose potential conversions faster than you can attract them. Next, the efficiency of your campaign relies heavily on your ability to fine-tune critical elements—every small adjustment can lead to significant improvements in your results. Lastly, understanding and implementing techniques to maximize conversions and ROI on platforms like Meta is essential. It's not just about spending money on ads; it's about investing in strategies that will pay off in the long run.

Navigating through this process may sound daunting, but fear not. The following step-by-step guide, dubbed **"The Converter's Compass"**, is designed to demystify the optimization process and set you on a clear path to achieving your advertising goals.

The Converter's Compass: A Step-by-Step Guide to Crushing Your Meta Ad Goals

Step 1: Optimize landing pages

Your landing page is often the first impression users get of your brand. Make it count by ensuring it's fully aligned with your campaign objectives. A seamless user experience, combined with compelling content and clear calls-to-action (CTAs), can significantly boost your conversion rates. Keep it as simple as possible—minimal form fields and lightning-fast loading times are your best friends here.

Step 2: Test different call-to-action (CTA) buttons

Never underestimate the power of a well-crafted CTA. Testing variations in wording, color, size, and placement can unveil what resonates best with your audience. Remember, the goal is to induce action, so make sure your CTAs are clear, compelling, and convey a sense of urgency.

Step 3: Improve ad copy

Polish your ad copy until it shines. It needs to be concise, yet powerful enough to grab attention and persuade. Incorporate social proof where possible to bolster credibility, and don't shy away from highlighting what makes your offer stand out.

Step 4: Optimize ad visuals

In the world of Meta ads, visuals can make or break your campaign. Test different formats—images, videos, carousels—to discover what captures your audience's attention best. High-quality, relevant imagery is not just appealing; it's compelling and can significantly drive engagement.

Step 5: Implement A/B testing

The beauty of digital advertising lies in its measurability. Utilize A/B testing to put different elements of your campaign against each other—be it ads, landing pages, or CTAs. This not only helps in identifying the most effective strategies but also aids in making data-driven decisions to optimize performance continually.

Step 6: Monitor key performance metrics

Keeping a vigilant eye on metrics such as click-through rates, conversion rates, and ROI is vital. These numbers are a treasure trove of insights, guiding you on what's working and what's not. Adjust your strategy based on these insights to steer your campaign toward peak performance.

Step 7: Refine targeting options

Meta offers a plethora of targeting options. Use data and campaign insights to continually refine your audience segments. Effective targeting is a precision tool—it's about reaching the right person, with the right message, at the right time.

Step 8: Optimize for mobile

With the majority of Meta users accessing the platform via mobile devices, optimizing for mobile is not optional; it's essential. Ensure your ads and landing pages offer a flawless mobile browsing experience to maximize engagement and conversions.

Envisioning and implementing these steps should not be a

one-off exercise **but rather a cyclic process of refinement and improvement**. Each cycle brings you closer to understanding your audience's preferences and how best to cater to them. *Remember, optimization is not a destination but a journey*—one that requires persistence, agility, and a keen eye for detail.

Through *"The Converter's Compass"*, you're equipped to navigate the ever-changing landscape of Meta advertising. By systematically applying these steps, you're not just aiming for incremental improvements; you're setting the stage for exponential growth. With a user-centric approach, meticulous campaign tuning, and a relentless pursuit of excellence, you're well on your way to transforming your Meta ad campaigns into unassailable engines of conversion.

Employ Strategies to Optimize Landing Pages, Calls-to-Action, and User Experience for Higher Conversion Rates

In the digital arena, optimizing landing pages is akin to setting the stage for a grand performance. The curtain rises the moment a potential customer arrives, and every element on the page plays a part in the unfolding drama. The goal? To guide the visitor towards the climax of this performance—

conversion. This necessitates a page that's not only aesthetically pleasing but also highly functional, loading quickly and displaying seamlessly across all devices.

Imagine walking into a store where the layout is chaotic, the sales pitch inconsistent, and the checkout process cumbersome. It's unlikely you'd proceed with a purchase. This scenario is comparable to a poorly designed landing page. Just as a shopper navigates through aisles, online visitors navigate through your landing page. The easier and more engaging this journey, the higher the likelihood of a conversion. Elements such as clear calls-to-action (CTAs), concise messaging, and an intuitive layout are not mere details—they are the very pathways that guide a visitor towards making a decision.

Furthermore, optimizing calls-to-action is not just about choosing the right words; it's about creating a sense of urgency and value that resonates with your audience. Testing different CTAs involves not just variations in verbiage but also in color, size, and placement on the page. It's about understanding the psychology of your potential customers and what drives them to take action.

Improving the overall user experience is both an art and a science. It involves a deep understanding of your audience's needs and behaviors, and crafting an experience that not only meets but exceeds their expectations. Fast page load times, mobile responsiveness, and easy navigation are no longer luxuries—they are expectations.

In essence, optimizing landing pages, calls-to-action, and user experience is about creating a clear, enticing path for your visitors to follow, leading them smoothly from interest to action.

The Journey to Campaign Efficiency: A Step-by-Step Guide

Step 1: Optimize Landing Pages

Begin by scrutinizing your landing pages through the lens of your campaign objectives. Each element, from design to content, should sing in harmony to offer a seamless, conversion-centered performance. Ensure your calls-to-action stand out bold and clear, like a guiding lighthouse, and minimize any form fields to just the essentials. It's all about reducing friction and speeding up the journey from arrival to conversion.

Step 2: Test Different Call-to-Action (CTA) Buttons

Embarking on a quest to find the most compelling CTAs involves experimentation and testing. It's a dance of words, colors, sizes, and positions, each variant echoing a different tone and motivation. The goal is to strike the right chord with your audience, prompting an immediate, irresistible urge to engage.

Step 3: Improve Ad Copy

Polishing your ad copy until it gleams with persuasion, relevance, and uniqueness is crucial. Each word should be chosen for its power to convince and convert, supported by the credibility of social proof. This ensures your message not only captures attention but also fosters trust.

Step 4: Optimize Ad Visuals

In the visual symphony of your ads, each element must play its part to captivate and engage. Testing different formats—images, videos, carousels—allows you to discover which compositions resonate most profoundly with your audience. High-quality, relevant visuals strike emotional chords, inviting deeper engagement.

Step 5: Implement A/B testing

A/B testing serves as the compass guiding your optimization efforts, revealing the paths that lead to peak performance. By systematically comparing variants of your ads, landing pages, and other elements, you unearth the combinations that spark the most conversions.

Step 6: Monitor Key Performance Metrics

Keeping a vigilant eye on performance metrics equips you with the insights needed to continuously refine your campaign. These indicators act as milestones on your journey, pointing out both achievements and areas ripe for improvement.

Step 7: Refine Targeting Options

As insights accumulate, refining your audience targeting becomes a dynamic process of adjustment and discovery. Peel away the layers of underperforming options to reveal the core audience segments most aligned with your message, continually refining to enhance relevance and impact.

Step 8: Optimize for Mobile

In a world where the mobile device is king, optimizing for mobile is not optional—it's imperative. Ensure your campaigns provide a frictionless, engaging experience on these ubiquitous devices, addressing the preferences and behaviors of the majority.

By following these steps meticulously, could we unlock the full potential of our campaigns, turning every click into a beacon leading towards conversion success?

Gaining Insights and Techniques

for Maximizing Conversions and ROI on Meta Platforms

The Framework for Elevated Conversions

In optimizing for Meta platforms, envision a toolkit specifically crafted for enhancing direct response campaigns—a meticulous blend of science and intuition. This toolkit, an Evaluation Framework, serves as a scaffold upon which successful campaigns are built and refined.

Objective Identification & KPI Selection

The foundation of this framework rests on the solid ground of clearly defined campaign objectives. With objectives in hand, selecting Key Performance Indicators (KPIs) comes next, mapping out the metrics that will serve as beacons of progress—engagement rates, conversion rates, and ROI. Like setting the destination in a navigation app, knowing precisely what you aim to achieve guides every decision that follows.

Data Collection & Analysis

Engaging with Meta's analytics tools unlocks a treasure trove of insights. This step is akin to conducting a meticulous excavation, where data points are unearthed and carefully examined to reveal the story beneath the surface. By adopting a systematic approach to collecting and analyzing data, you lay the groundwork for informed decision-making.

Structured A/B Testing

With the Evaluation Framework, A/B testing evolves from a mere tactic to a principled approach for incremental improvement. Testing variations in ad creatives, targeting parameters, and CTAs is like conducting experiments in a laboratory—each iteration brings you closer to discovering what truly resonates with your audience.

Prioritization Matrix

Resources, both time and money, are finite. The Prioritization Matrix within this framework helps allocate these precious commodities towards the optimization efforts most likely to yield significant returns. It's about betting wisely, not just betting more.

Interpreting Data for Decisions

The process of interpreting data is both an art and a science. It involves discerning patterns, understanding statistical significance, and avoiding the pitfalls of misinterpretation. This component ensures that decisions are not just data-informed but data-wise.

In sum, by employing this Evaluation Framework, businesses can systematically optimize their direct response campaigns on Meta platforms. It offers a

structured, scalable approach to enhancing every aspect of a campaign, culminating in maximized conversions and ROI.

By integrating strategies to optimize landing pages, fine-tuning key elements for better campaign results, and employing a structured approach to maximize conversions and ROI on Meta platforms, businesses can unlock unprecedented levels of success. This holistic approach not only elevates campaign performance but also positions brands to outwit algorithms, outmaneuver competitors, and outperform expectations.

Key Takeaways:

Optimization techniques are like the secret sauce that can take your Meta ad campaigns from good to exceptional. By **implementing strategies** to fine-tune your **landing pages, calls-to-action**, and **user experience**, you're setting yourself up for a **higher conversion rate** and a **better return on investment**.

Unlocking Success:

Remember, the devil is in the details when it comes to digital marketing. It's the **small tweaks** and **refinements** that can make a world of difference in your campaign's performance. **Optimizing** every aspect of your ad journey on Meta platforms is not just a suggestion; it's a **necessary step** towards achieving your goals.

Elevate Your Performance:

Don't underestimate the power of optimization. By continuously **testing**, **analyzing data**, and **fine-tuning** your approach, you're not just improving your campaigns; you're **winning the digital marketing game**. Stay committed to the process, and the results will speak for themselves.

So, as you move forward in your journey to conquer the digital realm, keep these optimization techniques close at hand. They are the keys that will unlock the full potential of your ads on Meta platforms.

Chapter 8: Analytics: The Navigational Compass for Campaigns

The early autumn breeze carried a scent of change through the small office on the upper floor of a bustling Chicago advertising agency. There, amidst walls lined with framed successes, sat Nicholas, a strategist whose glasses sat perennially on the edge of his nose, reflecting the glow of multiple monitors. Each screen was a porthole into the data-driven world he inhabited; a tableau of graphs, percentages, and predictive models. His fingers danced across the keyboard as if playing a sonata, crafting a symphony of campaigns molded by the logic of analytics tools.

As Nicholas carefully scrutinized the performance metrics of his latest campaign, the city's murmur seeped through his window, a subtle reminder of the countless individuals his work aimed to entice. His mind was a whirlpool of thoughts, churning with the critical need for continuous improvement. He knew that stagnation was a luxury afforded to none in the cutthroat terrain of advertising. It was this very pursuit of campaign optimization that sent ripples through his consciousness, as ideas ebbed and flowed like the tides influenced by the moon's pull.

He remembered a campaign from the past summer, one that started with a sparkle but fizzled out, like a firework lost in the daylight. He had not heeded the whispers of his analytics tools then; he had been so sure of his gut feeling. The memory stung him with a lesson well learned — in advertising, the heart must sometimes yield to the hard numbers.

Sipping his coffee, now lukewarm, Nicholas allowed the bitter taste to ground him back to the present. A coworker brushed past, leaving behind a trail of laughter and a few crumbs from the morning's pastries. It was a brief but human interruption, a stark contrast to his digital haven.

He delved once more into the realm of "Conquest Clicks," an initiative on Meta platforms that held promise. The stakes were high, and the need for precision was paramount. With each click tracked, each conversion analyzed, he fine-tuned the campaign, a painter adding deft brushstrokes to a masterpiece yet unseen.

Yet doubt, that old adversary, sometimes clouded his vision. Would the data lead him astray? Was there a hidden signal he was failing to see? Analytics was both his map and compass, but the terrain of human desire was often shrouded in mist.

As the shadows crept across his desk, Nicholas pondered the impending presentation to his client. Would they grasp the subtleties of his data-driven strategy? The numbers told a story, but could he narrate it in a way that resonated with both logic and emotion?

His day was far from over; his quest for improvement never ceased. And in the silence of his office, a question lingered, echoing off the walls — how does one balance the precision of data with the unpredictability of human behavior?

Navigating the digital seas of Meta advertising is a complex voyage—a mission where the winds are data streams, and your compass, advanced analytics tools, charts the course to untapped territories of opportunity. As part of your campaign mastery, understanding and utilizing these tools is not just advantageous; it's imperative for thriving in an environment where every click can conquer new frontiers.

The Alchemy of Analytics: Turning Data into Gold

In this digital age, analytics serve as the alchemists, transforming raw data into valuable insights that can steer your advertising campaigns toward success. Imagine having the power to not only see the results of your efforts in real time but also to understand why certain ads resonate with audiences and others fall flat. This is the reality when you harness advanced analytics tools. They allow you to peer beneath the surface of your campaigns, revealing the secrets of your successes and the lessons in your losses.

The first step in this alchemical process is to **set up your**

analytics tools properly. Selecting the right tools is crucial; they must align with your goals and integrate seamlessly with your Meta advertising accounts. Once set up, you embark on a journey of defining what success looks like for your campaigns. Key performance metrics become your star constellations, guiding you by their relative positions and brightness in the digital sky.

Monitoring real-time data reveals the immediate impacts of your campaigns. It's akin to navigating by observing the ocean's current; you can adjust your course promptly to catch the most favorable winds. Regularly checking these metrics ensures you're not drifting off course—or worse, heading toward an iceberg field of underperforming ads.

Data segmentation then lets you drill down into the specifics. Just as a cartographer segments a map into regions to provide more detailed insights, this step enables you to analyze particular audience segments or ad formats more closely. It's about identifying which territories are ripe for exploration and which are proving barren.

Attribution modeling and **funnel analysis** serve to further refine your understanding. They unravel the complexities of customer journeys, showing you the paths most traveled and the obstacles that impede progress. This knowledge empowers you to make the necessary adjustments, ensuring a smoother voyage for your prospective customers and a more profitable outcome for your campaigns.

Finally, compiling custom reports and dashboards crystallizes your findings. It's the moment of truth where data transforms into actionable intelligence. These reports not only guide your immediate decisions but also inform your long-term strategy, ensuring that every adjustment is a step toward more efficient and effective advertising.

Charting a Course with Confidence

Utilizing advanced analytics tools follows a sequence that gradually unveils deeper insights and empowers data-driven decisions. It begins with establishing a foundation through proper setup and metric definition, progresses through monitoring and segmentation for nuanced understanding, and culminates in applying sophisticated modeling techniques for optimization. Each step is a stride toward mastery, transforming analytics from a mere tool into a strategic ally.

Your mission, should you choose to accept it, involves making informed decisions that refine your advertising strategy with precision. It's about not merely sailing the digital seas but mastering them, ensuring that every wave you ride and every breeze that fills your sails is part of a calculated voyage towards unparalleled success.

Remember, the measure of a successful voyage isn't just in reaching your destination but in the treasures you discover along the way. With analytics as your navigational compass, each campaign becomes an expedition that uncovers insights and strategies that are worth their weight in gold. The cycle of continuous improvement that analytics fosters propels you forward, ensuring that with each campaign, you are not just navigating the digital landscape but conquering it.

Utilize Advanced Analytics Tools for Comprehensive Tracking and Analysis of Campaigns

Navigating the vast ocean of digital marketing requires more than just a good instinct or a well-crafted ad; it demands precision navigation tools. Advanced analytics tools are the sextants and compasses of the digital advertising age, enabling marketers to chart a path through the data and steer their campaigns toward success. Without these tools, advertisers are adrift in a sea of guesswork and assumption.

Taking the analogy of sea navigation further, consider your campaign as a ship setting sail. The utilization of advanced analytics tools is akin to plotting your course with precision maps, continuously adjusting to the winds and currents of consumer behavior and market trends. These tools help to illuminate the murky waters of digital advertising, revealing the most efficient routes to your desired outcomes.

Modern analytics platforms offer a comprehensive view into the performance of advertising campaigns. They track a variety of metrics such as click-through rates, engagement levels, conversion rates, and more. This data is invaluable for understanding which aspects of a campaign are working and which are not. However, the sheer volume of data available can be overwhelming. This is where the real skill lies: not just in the gathering of data, but in the interpretation and application of that data to improve campaign performance.

The process of analysis doesn't stop with a one-time setup. It's an ongoing cycle of monitoring, testing, learning, and adjusting. Every piece of data collected serves as a feedback loop, informing the next decision and refinement to the campaign. This iterative process is what leads to continuous improvement and, ultimately, to achieving and surpassing campaign objectives.

The key to steering your campaigns towards success is mastering the use of advanced analytics tools for comprehensive tracking and analysis.

The Compass Points To Data-Driven Decision Making

Imagine embarking on an unknown territory with only a compass in hand. The metaphorical compass in the realm of advertising is the data-driven decision-making process. It's not just about having the right tools; it's about understanding the direction the data points you in and having the confidence to follow that path.

The Steps to Navigate By Data:

Step 1: Set up analytics tools

The foundational step is selecting and properly setting up the analytics tools that best meet your campaign's goals. Think of this as choosing the right type of compass for the journey. Whether it's Google Analytics, Facebook Pixel, or another platform, the correct integration of these tools with your advertising accounts is crucial for accurate tracking.

Step 2: Define key performance metrics

Identifying the key performance indicators (KPIs) is akin to knowing your landmarks. These metrics, such as conversion rates or click-through rates, serve as beacons to gauge the success of your campaign. Setting clear benchmarks for these metrics provides a tangible target to aim for.

Step 3: Monitor real-time data

Constant monitoring of your campaign's performance is like keeping a vigilant eye on the horizon. This ensures you can quickly identify and adjust your strategies in response to emerging trends or shifts in consumer behavior.

Step 4: Segment data for analysis

Dividing your campaign data into segments provides a closer look at specific areas, allowing for a more nuanced understanding of performance across different audience demographics or ad formats. This is comparable to zooming in on particular features of the landscape to find the most effective path forward.

Step 5: Utilize attribution modeling

Attribution modeling helps pinpoint what elements of your campaign are driving results. Similar to recognizing the influence of winds and currents on your journey, this step reveals the touchpoints that are contributing most to conversions.

Step 6: Implement funnel analysis

Understanding and optimizing each stage of your conversion funnel is crucial. This is like ensuring every part of your ship is seaworthy, minimizing leaks (drop-offs), and streamlining the path to conversion.

Step 7: Create custom reports and dashboards

Custom reports and dashboards allow you to visualize and share your campaign's performance in a way that is most relevant and actionable. This equips your crew (team) with the insights needed to make informed decisions.

Step 8: Make data-driven decisions

This final step circles back to the essence of the process:

using the insights gained to refine and adjust your strategies. Continuous analysis and application of data are what drive a successful journey.

Could the key to unlocking unprecedented campaign success lie in the next pie chart or data trend you analyze?

Continuous Improvement Through Performance Analytics

Continuous improvement in advertising campaigns is like sharpening a blade; the more you hone it, the more effective it becomes. Performance analytics play the role of the whetstone in this process, providing the friction necessary to trim away inefficiencies and enhance the edge of your campaigns.

In the realm of digital advertising, the landscape is ever-changing. New trends emerge, consumer behaviors shift, and competitors adapt their strategies. In this dynamic environment, resting on laurels is not an option. Utilizing performance analytics is how advertisers stay agile, making small, data-backed adjustments that cumulatively lead to significant improvements over time.

Consider the journey of a campaign from inception to completion as a series of experiments. Each ad, each target audience, and each piece of creative is a hypothesis being tested. Performance analytics provide the results of these tests, highlighting what works and what doesn't. With this information, campaigns can be iteratively refined, improving their effectiveness with each iteration.

Ultimately, the true power of analytics is not just in the numbers themselves but in the insights they reveal. It's about understanding the story behind the metrics, the why behind the what. This deep understanding is what enables advertisers to move beyond reaction to anticipation, preparing for shifts in the market before they happen and keeping their campaigns one step ahead.

Uniting the utilization of advanced analytics, making data-driven decisions, and fostering continuous improvement through performance analytics serves as the guiding star for elevating campaign efficiency. This cohesive strategy ensures that your campaigns are not only optimized for today but are also poised for enduring success in the dynamic landscape of digital advertising.

Take Your Campaigns to New Heights

As we near the end of this chapter, it's vital to underscore the significance of what we've discussed. **Utilizing advanced analytics tools** is not just an option; it's a necessity in today's digital advertising landscape. The ability to **track and analyze performance metrics** sets the foundation for successful campaigns.

By making **informed decisions** based on concrete data, you have the power to shape the trajectory of your advertising strategies. This isn't a guessing game—it's about utilizing insights to refine and optimize your campaigns for maximum impact.

Continuous improvement isn't just a buzzword; it's the **key to unlocking efficiency** in your advertising efforts. In the world of digital marketing, where algorithms shift and trends evolve rapidly, keeping a close eye on performance analytics is what sets apart the average from the exceptional.

Embrace the Data Journey

As you move forward in your advertising endeavors, remember that **knowledge is power**. The more you delve into the analytics of your campaigns, the clearer your path becomes. Every data point is a piece of the puzzle, guiding you towards smarter decisions and more successful outcomes.

Be proactive in your approach to analytics. Don't just collect data for the sake of it; use it as your compass, guiding you through the ever-changing landscape of digital advertising on Meta platforms.

Drive Success Through Insights

In the realm of online advertising, **data reigns supreme**. Your ability to harness the power of analytics and translate insights into action is what will set you apart from the competition.

Stay agile in your strategies, always seeking ways to refine and optimize based on what the data tells you. Remember, the journey to campaign success is paved with analytics—embrace them, leverage them, and watch your efforts soar to new heights.

Chapter 9: The Roadmap to Mastery on Meta Platforms

Winter in Chicago is a silent poet. Snow blankets the sidewalks, turning footprints into stanzas of the day's perambulations. Anna perches by her office window, staring into the frosted canvas that stretches down Michigan Avenue. Inside, her office breathes warmth and familiarity, the gentle hum of computers collaborating with the intermittent sighs of her colleagues.

She contemplates the ad campaign laid bare on her screen, tattered edges of hope fraying with every click that doesn't convert. Her mind wades into the manuscript of 'Conquest Clicks', its words promising the revelations of a digital messiah. She had devoured its contents, letting the strategies seep into the parched cracks of her doubt. Armed with tactics just shy of familiarity, she yearned for the certainty that her investment in the Meta platforms would bear fruit.

A notification interrupts her musings, an analytic beacon: declining conversion rates blink at her with a cold indifference. Fingers tap on the keyboard with a nervous energy, adjusting audiences, refining copy. She thinks back to chapters on insight, on clarity, and the methodical construction of a campaign that speaks. Her reflection upon the screen is pale, a ghost caught in the machinations of targeted algorithms and consumer profiles.

Her colleague James strides in, breathless from the cold that snaps at his heels. "How's the battlefield today?" he asks, his eyes narrowing with the common bond of those who seek triumph in the trenches of digital marketing. She shares her plight, the ROI not yet conquered, response rates that mimic the silent snowfall outside. He listens, nods, and recounts tales from his own skirmish with the online behemoths. Together, they lay plans infused by the doctrine of 'Conquest Clicks.'

As evening encroaches and the sky melts into shades of orange and bruised purple, she looks again at her campaign metrics. There's a small uptick, a whisper that suggests she might be closing in on success. Hope flutters, a moth drawn to the incandescence of potential. The office quiets, and in the thickening silence, her mind wanders through the myriad possible futures paved by clicks and conversions.

Outside, the world turns unabated, indifferent to the dramas unfolding on pixelated screens. And as the city lights blur with the onset of a night that carries its own secrets, one wonders: can the structured roadmap of 'Conquest Clicks' truly navigate the chaos of human desire?

Unleashing the Power of Strategic Meta

Advertising

In a digital landscape where every click could be the difference between profit and loss, mastering Meta platforms for direct response advertising is not just an advantage; it's a necessity. The essence of success in this realm isn't found in fleeting trends or top-level metrics but in deeply understanding and leveraging the intricate tools and data Meta offers. This is where the roadmap to mastery unfolds, guiding the way through the complexities of digital advertising with a clear, structured approach. This isn't about throwing strategies at the wall to see what sticks; it's about making each move with intention, precision, and insight.

The first step on this journey is a **commitment to a structured approach**. The digital world is vast and constantly evolving, but that doesn't mean navigating it should feel like wandering in the dark. By harnessing a meticulous, step-by-step strategy tailored for Meta's platforms, advertisers can sidestep common pitfalls and accelerate their path to success. This approach isn't merely theoretical; it's a practical blueprint that, when followed, paves the way for achieving tangible, measurable improvements in campaign performance.

Implementing **clear strategies and actionable insights** is the cornerstone of this process. Meta's array of platforms, each with its unique audience and algorithms, demands a nuanced understanding. Strategies that fly on Facebook might falter on Instagram, and vice versa. This segment of the roadmap underscores the importance of agility and specificity in campaign design and execution. Through a detailed exploration of platform-specific features, advertising formats, and audience targeting options, readers will gain the knowledge needed to craft campaigns that resonate with their intended audience.

Achieving **higher ROI and advertising success** is the ultimate destination. The digital advertising realm is a competitive arena, where every bit of efficiency and optimization can make a difference. By adhering to the guidance outlined in the roadmap, advertisers are not just aiming to improve their campaigns in isolation; they're seeking to outwit algorithms, outmaneuver competitors, and outperform market expectations. This isn't just about better advertising; it's about building a superior, more resilient digital marketing strategy.

Throughout this discussion, remember the value of learning from both successes and setbacks. Digital advertising on Meta is as much an art as it is a science. Crafting compelling ads, pinpointing the perfect audience, and optimizing for peak performance are skills honed over time. Each campaign offers a wealth of data—learn from it. Analyze what worked, discern what didn't, and refine your approach accordingly. This iterative process is crucial to mastering the craft.

Moreover, embracing technological advancements and platform updates is vital. Meta continuously evolves, introducing new features and adjusting algorithms. Staying informed and adaptable ensures your strategies remain relevant and effective. Embrace these changes as opportunities to innovate and lead in the space, not as hurdles to overcome.

By following the roadmap laid out in this comprehensive guide, you're not just learning to navigate the complex world of Meta advertising—you're mastering it. This journey is about more than clicks and conversions; it's about building a robust, dynamic approach to digital marketing that drives real business outcomes. Armed with structured strategies, actionable insights, and a commitment to continuous improvement, the path to mastery is within reach.

Following a Structured Approach

To unravel the intricacies of direct response advertising on Meta platforms, it's essential to first lay a strong foundation. This means understanding the basics: from recognizing what direct response advertising entails to identifying the various Meta platforms and how they operate. The primary objective here is not just to catch the eye but to prompt an action - be it a click, a purchase, or a sign-up. This principle drives the very core of successful advertising campaigns on such social media giants.

Think of mastering direct response advertising on Meta platforms as gardening. You wouldn't start planting without first understanding the soil type, climate, and what plants thrive under specific conditions. Similarly, diving into Meta advertising without a structured approach is akin to planting seeds haphazardly and hoping for the best. The structured approach is your gardening plan, detailing where, when, and how to plant to ensure a bountiful harvest.

To navigate through the complex landscape of Meta advertising, adopting a structured approach involves building your knowledge progressively. It starts with grasping the basic concepts and tools available on Meta platforms and understanding how to use these tools effectively. Knowing your audience and how to target them accurately is another crucial step. This doesn't happen overnight but involves ongoing learning and adjustment based on analytics and campaign performance.

Utilizing a structured approach allows you to systematically test and refine your advertising efforts. By establishing clear objectives and benchmarks, you can iteratively improve upon your campaigns. This systematic experimentation not only enhances your understanding of what resonates with your audience but also helps you to optimize your budget effectively.

A structured approach to mastering direct response advertising on Meta is crucial for laying a strong foundation and ensuring long-term success.

Implementing Strategies for Success

Direct response advertising in the convoluted digital landscape requires more than just a good understanding of platforms; it demands a strategic approach. This involves knowing what you want to achieve and planning how to get there, incorporating clear strategies and actionable insights. These strategies could range from choosing the right campaign objectives to creating compelling ad content that resonates with your target audience.

Engaging your audience effectively means talking to them in a language they understand and offering them something of value. It's not just about shouting into the void with generic messages. Imagine trying to navigate a dense forest without a map or compass; similarly, stepping into digital advertising without a strategic plan is likely to lead you off course.

Incorporating clear, actionable insights into your strategy is akin to having a GPS and a map in the aforementioned forest. It involves gathering data, interpreting it correctly, and then using this information to make informed decisions about your advertising efforts. This could mean adjusting your targeting criteria, refining your ad copy, or altering your budget allocation based on what the data tells you.

Feedback loops are an integral part of this process. By setting up mechanisms for regularly reviewing and adjusting your strategies based on campaign performance, you foster a culture of continuous improvement. This iterative process, much like refining a recipe with each attempt, ensures that your advertising efforts become more effective over time.

But how does one keep this strategy flexible enough to adapt to the ever-changing landscape of digital advertising? It's about staying informed, being ready to pivot, and always being curious. The digital world is not static; new platforms emerge, algorithms change, and consumer behaviors evolve. Staying ahead means embracing these changes, learning from them, and integrating new insights into your strategy.

How can you ensure your strategy remains adaptable and responsive to the fast-paced digital advertising environment?

Towards Advertising Success

The Conquest Clicks Mastery Framework

Achieving higher ROI and advertising success is not a matter of chance but a result of adhering to the guidance offered in the Conquest Clicks Mastery Framework. This process model outlines a phased approach to developing competency in direct response advertising on Meta, breaking down the journey into manageable, actionable steps.

Initial Assessment Phase

The journey begins with an evaluation of your current knowledge base and capabilities. It's like taking stock of your tools before embarking on a construction project. You assess what skills you already possess and identify the areas where you need improvement. This phase sets the stage for targeted learning, ensuring that the subsequent steps are as efficient and effective as possible.

Foundational Knowledge Acquisition

Following the assessment, the focus shifts to building a solid grounding in the essentials of Meta's advertising ecosystem. This includes understanding the different platforms under the Meta umbrella, mastering targeting options, creating compelling ad creatives, and interpreting analytics. It's the equivalent of laying the foundation for your construction project; without this base, any additional work is unlikely to stand the test of time.

Application and Practice

With a solid foundation in place, the next step involves applying this knowledge through creating and managing campaign simulations. This phase allows for experimentation in a controlled setting, enabling you to refine your approach based on real-world scenarios or case studies. Think of it as building a model structure before constructing the actual building. This safe environment fosters learning and adaptation without the high stakes of live campaigns.

Reflective Practices and Feedback Mechanisms

An integral part of the model is the incorporation of reflective practices and feedback mechanisms. After each simulation or real campaign, taking the time to evaluate what worked and what didn't allows for continuous improvement. This is akin to reviewing the blueprints and making adjustments after each model structure is built, ensuring that the final construction is as close to perfection as possible.

Mastery

Finally, the framework culminates in mastery, where you are tasked with designing and implementing a comprehensive direct response campaign from scratch. Leveraging all the learnings from the book and using advanced techniques, this phase challenges you to navigate algorithm changes and platform complexities. It's the moment where you move from building model structures to constructing a skyscraper, applying every skill and insight you've garnered along the way.

The Conquest Clicks Mastery Framework is a blueprint for success, guiding advertisers from foundational understanding to proficient application and mastery of direct response marketing on Meta platforms.

The Pathway to Success

As we bring this chapter to a close, remember that **following a structured approach** to mastering direct response advertising on Meta platforms is key to your success. The strategies and insights provided in this guide are your tools for navigating the complexities of digital advertising with confidence. By implementing the recommendations outlined in this book, you are equipping yourself with the means to achieve **higher ROI** and advertising success in a shorter time frame.

Embark on Your Journey

Now that you have gained a deeper understanding of the roadmap to mastery on Meta platforms, it's time to put your knowledge into action. **Implement clear strategies** and actionable insights to navigate the world of digital advertising with finesse. Stay true to the guidance offered in this book, and you will undoubtedly see the fruits of your labor in your campaigns.

A Roadmap to Excellence

As you move forward, keep in mind that **adhering to the principles** in this guide is your pathway to conquering the challenges of digital advertising. With a commitment to honing your skills, you are well on your way to achieving unparalleled success in your advertising endeavors. Stay focused, stay determined, and let the journey to mastery unfold before you.

Chapter 10: Assembling the Arsenal for Advertising Success

She moved through the morning haze; the city was a canvas barely touched by the light. Emilia's heart held a rhythm set by the routine of her early commute, a rhythm disrupted today by a troubling thought - the rumble of a challenge she had yet to overcome.

It was the advertisement campaign she had launched on the Meta platform. For weeks, the numbers had come in flat, a reflection of some missing element in her strategy. As a digital marketer, she knew the intricacies involved - targeting the right audience, crafting messages that clicked, optimizing every stage of the customer journey - yet somewhere, there was a disconnect.

Her shoes clicked on the pavement, echoing off the storefronts of Sixth Avenue, each step a reminder of the resolve she needed to muster. She had studied the courses, attended the webinars, and internalized the anthem of 'Conquest Clicks' - their roadmap was thorough, but applying it in the real-world was a different beast. The problem lay not in knowing, but in execution. This was no ancient text to be deciphered, no secret code; it was a puzzle where all the pieces were given, yet the assembly was hers to master.

The cool morning air brushed her face as she let her thoughts mingle with the sounds of the waking city. Perhaps, she considered, the issue was in the creative execution - the vibrant ads she envisioned were dimmed in the labyrinth of online noise. Maybe the message was right, but the audience? Not quite. She recalled the webinars - we're aiming for a sharpshooter's approach, not that of a scattergun. Precision, targeting, understanding user behavior - these were the tenets that floated to the forefront of her contemplation.

Emilia reached her office, greeted by the familiarity of her desk, the persistent glow of her computer screen, and promises of potential. Today she would tweak, test, and transform. Today the campaign would shift - it had to. A sip of water, a deep breath, and she dived into the analytics; numbers and graphs greeted her, a chorus of data waiting to be harmonized into success.

The street outside mellowed to a midday murmur. As her fingers danced over the keyboard, adjusting demographics, refining ad copy, realigning budgets with meticulous precision, the campaign began to breathe anew. A surge in clicks, a spike in engagement - signs of life.

Yet these were mere steps on a longer path, a path strewn with ever-evolving challenges. The horizon held untold updates, new algorithms, emerging trends. In this dance of digits and decisions, could Emilia's tenacity keep pace with the relentless march of technology? Or would the machine outpace the human touch?

Unlocking the Mastery of Meta Advertising

The realm of direct response advertising on Meta platforms is akin to navigating a labyrinth; only those armed with a comprehensive understanding, precision in execution, and an adaptable strategy emerge victorious. In the treacherous waters of Meta advertising, where algorithms change as unpredictably as the wind, the need for a well-assembled arsenal is not just beneficial—it's imperative. This is where the essence of "Conquest Clicks" comes into play, offering not just insights but a roadmap to mastering the complexities of this digital advertising arena.

Success in this domain isn't rooted in fluke or sheer luck; it's the result of meticulous planning, understanding the nuanced game of targeting, creative optimization, and conversion strategies. Just as a craftsman needs the right tools to bring a vision to life, **a marketer needs the right skills, tactics, and strategies to influence the desired audience action.** This is not about casting a wide net; it's about precision fishing in the vast ocean of digital users, identifying and captivating your ideal catch.

One of the key learning objectives of this pivotal chapter is to furnish readers with a crystal-clear understanding of what these essential skills, tactics, and strategies are. Consider this: knowledge of your toolbox is just the start; knowing when, how, and where to deploy each tool is what sets the master apart from the amateur. By drilling down into areas such as advanced targeting mechanisms, creative best practices tailored for the Meta landscape, and the intricacies of conversion optimization, you begin to paint not just with broad strokes but with the detail and precision necessary for impactful results.

Moreover, achieving this level of mastery isn't just about enhancing individual campaign performance; it's about driving fundamental improvements across all advertising efforts on Meta platforms. Imagine being able to consistently *outwit algorithms, outmaneuver competitors, and outperform expectations*. This vision is achievable, grounded in understanding the why and how of each action and reaction within the advertising ecosystem of Meta.

To thread the needle further, "Conquest Clicks" offers a structured, methodical roadmap designed to navigate the complex web of direct response advertising on Meta. This structured approach is akin to a navigator charting a course through stormy seas, with each chapter building upon the last, culminating in this comprehensive guide to not just survive but to thrive in the Meta advertising world.

Within these pages lies the synthesis of the entire book's

themes, tying together the golden threads of mastering ad creation, campaign management, and optimization strategies. The core problem this roadmap solves is significant; it overcomes the challenge of constant, often abrupt changes in Meta's advertising ecosystem. The end goal? To usher readers into a realm where they can create, manage, and optimize their campaigns to drive conversions and achieve their business objectives effectively and efficiently.

In essence, this chapter isn't merely another segment of the book—it's the capstone, the moment where all learned principles coalesce into a clear, actionable strategy. Armed with the insights and wisdom distilled through "Conquest Clicks," you stand on the threshold of transforming your Meta advertising endeavors. Let this be your invitation to step beyond the threshold and into a world of advertising success crafted by mastery, strategy, and relentless pursuit of excellence.

Succeeding in the dynamic realm of Meta's advertising platforms is akin to mastering a complex yet rewarding board game. Just as in any game, there are rules to learn, strategies to devise, and skills to hone. At its core, the success formula revolves around a comprehensive understanding of essential skills, tactics, and strategies. These encompass knowing your audience with precision, crafting messages that resonate deeply, and leveraging Meta's robust analytical tools to optimize for performance. Knowing how to blend these elements efficiently can turn advertising campaigns from mediocre to monumental.

The landscape of Meta advertising is ever-changing, much like the weather in a bustling city. One day, it's all sunny skies with your ads performing well, and the next, algorithm changes bring in clouds, demanding a nimble response. The key skill here is adaptability - understanding that what works today might need tweaking tomorrow. This constant evolution requires advertisers to be lifelong learners of the platform's intricacies, with a zeal to experiment and a patience to iterate.

Diving into tactics, imagine each ad campaign as a seed. You need to plant it in the right soil (target audience), give it the right amount of sunlight (engaging content), and regularly water it (optimize performance) to see it bloom (achieve desired outcomes). This analogy exemplifies the tactical side of Meta advertising – selecting the right audience segments, creating compelling ad creatives, and continually refining campaigns based on performance data. Mastering these tactics is crucial for any advertiser aiming for success.

Strategically, it's all about the big picture, envisioning the garden you want to cultivate over time. Strategy in Meta advertising involves setting clear objectives, aligning business goals with marketing efforts, and mapping out a journey that turns prospects into loyal customers. It's a meticulous process of planning, execution, and scaling, all while keeping a close eye on the competitive landscape and market trends.

In a nutshell, achieving success on Meta platforms is a multifaceted endeavor, requiring a mix of skills, tactics, and strategies. It demands both the creativity to engage audiences and the analytical acumen to iterate based on data-driven insights. **Mastering these elements is the foundation of advertising success on Meta.**

Achieving Impact Through Mastery

To truly impact the business bottom line, mastery in targeting, creative best practices, and conversion optimization becomes non-negotiable. Targeting on Meta platforms allows you to pinpoint your audience with surgical precision. It's not about casting a wide net; it's more akin to weaving a web where your ideal customers can't help but get caught. This level of targeting efficiency means understanding audience behaviors, preferences, and demographics to an extent few platforms can match.

Creative best practices on Meta are not just about making things look pretty; they're about grabbing attention in a sea of content. It's about storytelling in a way that not only captures interest but also beckons interaction. The real art lies in blending persuasive messaging with visual appeal, creating an irresistible pull towards your offering. In this realm, the mantra is simple: Be bold, be engaging, and always be testing.

When it comes to conversion optimization, think of it as fine-tuning a race car. Every adjustment, no matter how minor, can shave off milliseconds that, in the end, define victory. In advertising terms, it's about refining every element of your campaign—from the call-to-action to the landing page—ensuring that every touchpoint is optimized to guide the user smoothly along the conversion path.

Yet, while these components are critical, integrating them harmoniously into a cohesive strategy is where the magic happens. It's the difference between playing single notes and composing a symphony—the latter resonates deeper and stays with the audience long after the performance.

Rhetorical devices, like questions, can provoke thought and challenge assumptions. One might ask, "Is our brand truly connecting with our audience, or are we just another voice in the cacophony?" This introspection can lead to a reevaluation of strategies, ensuring efforts are not just seen but felt.

How can integrating these methodologies into your advertising strategies transform your approach and yield unprecedented outcomes?

Roadmap to Excellence

Implementing the structured roadmap offered by "Conquest Clicks" for excelling in direct response advertising on Meta platforms is akin to embarking on a guided hike through treacherous yet exhilarating terrain. The guide knows every twist and turn, ensuring you can focus on the scenery – in this case, the growth and success of your advertising efforts – without losing your way.

The initial step in this roadmap involves setting clear, measurable goals. Just as a hiker needs a destination, advertisers need objectives that define success. Whether it's increasing website traffic, boosting sales, or enhancing brand awareness, clarity in goals sets the direction for all subsequent actions.

Next, understanding the terrain is essential, which in this context means comprehensively analyzing your target audience. It involves delving deep into demographics, interests, and online behaviors, much like studying a map before setting out. This knowledge enables the creation of highly targeted ad campaigns that resonate personally with viewers, much more effectively than generic advertising could.

The journey continues with crafting compelling ad creatives. This is where creativity meets strategy. You not only have to attract attention but also inspire action. Each ad is a stepping stone on the path to conversion, designed with both aesthetic appeal and strategic elements to guide viewers toward your desired action.

Finally, the roadmap emphasizes continual optimization and learning. The terrain of Meta advertising is constantly shifting, and what leads to success one day may not the next. Regularly analyzing campaign performance, testing different approaches, and being willing to pivot strategies are crucial for staying on course and reaching the summit of advertising success.

By developing a comprehensive understanding of essential skills, mastering targeted and creative practices, and following a structured approach to campaign management, advertisers can unlock the full potential of Meta platforms for direct response success.

Embracing Mastery in Direct Response Advertising

Success in direct response advertising on Meta platforms hinges on the mastery of various skills, tactics, and strategies. Throughout this chapter, we delved into the essential components necessary to excel in the ever-evolving landscape of digital advertising. From advanced targeting to creative best practices and conversion optimization, each element plays a pivotal role in crafting high-impact campaigns that yield tangible results. **By honing these crucial areas, advertisers can navigate the complexities of Meta platforms with confidence and finesse.**

Navigating the Road to Success

Mastering the skills outlined in this chapter serves as the foundation for conquering the challenges of direct response advertising on Meta platforms. The roadmap provided in this book offers a structured approach to elevate your advertising prowess and thrive in the competitive digital space. **By following this roadmap diligently, you equip yourself with the tools necessary to outwit algorithms, outmaneuver competitors, and exceed expectations.**

A Pathway to Excellence

As you embark on your journey to unlock the secrets of direct response success on Meta, remember that mastery is cultivated through dedication and practice. The diverse strategies and insights shared in this book pave the way for you to conquer the complexities of digital advertising within a span of six months. **By implementing these proven methods and staying attuned to industry trends, you position yourself for sustained success in the dynamic realm of Meta advertising.**

In mastering the art of direct response advertising on Meta platforms, you have armed yourself with the knowledge and expertise to navigate the intricacies of digital marketing with confidence. The transformative power of honing your skills in targeting, creativity, and optimization equips you to craft compelling campaigns that resonate with your audience and drive meaningful results. **Through perseverance and a commitment to continuous learning, you are primed to achieve new heights of success in the realm of online advertising.**

Epilogue

The Dawn of Direct Response Dominance

As we draw the curtains on this journey together, it's momentous to realize the ground we've covered. Through the valleys of uncertainty and the mountains of algorithm complexities, you've marched on, armed with an arsenal of strategies and insights that promise to elevate your Meta ad mastery. This isn't just the end of a rewarding expedition; it's the beginning of a conquest, where you outwit, outmaneuver, and outperform every expectation set before you.

Imagine weaving through the fabric of Meta's ever-evolving landscape, your campaigns not just surviving but thriving amidst the chaos. This isn't a distant dream, but a living, breathing reality you can achieve. Every chapter, every strategy, and every insight shared here has one purpose: to transform you into a maven of direct response advertising in a world where attention is the hardest currency to earn.

Boldly implementing the strategies detailed in this book will not only amplify your campaigns but also refine your understanding of what it means to truly connect with your audience on Meta platforms. It's about igniting conversations, fostering relationships, and ultimately, compelling your audience to take action.

Bringing Our Conquest to Reality

The essence of everything discussed boils down to actionable application in the real world. Whether you're a digital marketer at the cusp of innovation or a business owner determined to skyrocket your online presence, the principles laid out across these pages are your blueprint to success.

Consider this a masterclass in navigating the digital landscape, where agility and adaptability are your best allies. The core concepts—ranging from dissecting algorithms to crafting irresistible ad creatives, and from precision targeting to relentless optimization—are the building blocks of your fortress. **Use these insights to construct campaigns that not only captivate but convert.**

A Spectrum of Strategies at Your Fingertips

Reflecting on our journey, it's clear that mastering Meta advertising is no mere feat of luck; it's a meticulously calculated endeavor. We ventured through the intricacies of algorithm mastery, untangling the web of engagement signals to position your content favorably. We delved into competitor analysis, arming you with the knowledge to anticipate market movements and position your brand as the apex predator in your niche.

The discoveries shared on A/B testing weren't just about tweaking colors or headlines; they were about embracing a philosophy of constant evolution, where every data point guides your trajectory towards unassailable success.

Lighting Your Path Forward

Now, as you stand on the precipice of advertising greatness, the question isn't whether you can rise to the occasion; it's how far beyond it you're willing to soar. The insights and tactics detailed here are your map, but your ambition is the compass that will guide you through uncharted territories.

Embrace experimentation with the confidence of a seasoned navigator. Let the landscapes of Meta's platforms be your laboratory, where every test, every tweak, and every insight gleaned catapults you closer to your goals. Remember, in the dynamic realm of digital advertising, stagnation is akin to regression. The creed of the conqueror is to adapt, innovate, and triumph.

A Humble Nod to the Horizon

Despite the depth we've explored together, the digital marketing odyssey is never truly complete. The Meta ecosystem will continue to morph, presenting new challenges but also new opportunities. Let this book be your anchor, but never let it tether you from venturing beyond its pages.

In your hands, you hold a compendium of knowledge, ripe for application and ripe for expansion through your unique experiences and discoveries. The realm of further research, particularly in emerging trends and platform innovations, beckons. Heed its call, for in it lies the potential for even greater mastery and success.

Our Parting Sentiment

As we part ways, remember: the essence of conquest isn't merely in victory but in the relentless pursuit of excellence. Your journey from here is a testament to your commitment to not just participate in the digital arena but to dominate it.

May the strategies, insights, and wisdom imparted here serve as your steadfast allies. Let each campaign be a battle won, not just in clicks and conversions, but in the hearts and minds of your audience.

"The secret of change is to focus all of your energy not on fighting the old, but on building the new." - Socrates

This quote encapsulates the spirit of our shared journey. In the dynamic dance of digital advertising, let us not merely adjust to the rhythm of change but lead it, crafting the future with intrepid hearts and innovative minds.

www.ingramcontent.com/pod-product-compliance
Lightning Source LLC
Chambersburg PA
CBHW050307230526
45471CB00005B/2068